Apprentices and Eyewitnesses

Creative Liturgies for
Incarnational Worship:
Ash Wednesday to Ascension Day

Chris Thorpe

CANTERBURY
PRESS
Norwich

First published in 2019 by the Canterbury Press Norwich
Editorial office
3rd Floor, Invicta House
108–114 Golden Lane
London EC1Y 0TG, UK
www.canterburypress.co.uk

Canterbury Press is an imprint of Hymns Ancient & Modern Ltd
(a registered charity)

H
Y Ancient
M
N &Modern
S

Hymns Ancient & Modern® is a registered trademark of
Hymns Ancient & Modern Ltd
13A Hellesdon Park Road, Norwich,
Norfolk NR6 5DR, UK

Scripture quotations are from the New Revised Standard Version of the
Bible, Anglicized Edition, copyright © 1989, 1995 by the Division of
Christian Education of the National Council of the Churches of Christ in
the USA. Used by permission. All rights reserved.

British Library Cataloguing in Publication data

A catalogue record for this book is available
from the British Library

978 1-78622-110-0

Typeset by Regent Typesetting Ltd
Printed and bound in Great Britain by
CPI Group (UK) Ltd

Contents

Dedicated to
Sarah, Sophie and Jake, to Rachel and Theo

Introduction
What is Incarnational Worship?

How can we connect with a generation of people who are un-familiar with the Christian story, and have lost touch with the language of faith? How can we break through the carapace of our own over-familiarity with words and traditions that have become routine? When much of our liturgy can seem wordy and doctrinal, designed to be understood rather than felt, how can we move from head to heart?

These acts of worship start from a different place. They start with our experience of human life, using language that does not rely on religious familiarity and formulation. This worship starts with the joys and sorrows of our lives in relationship, as com-munities, and in the wider world. It ends with an opportunity to offer ourselves, engaging wholeheartedly with the process of becoming the good news we proclaim.

The incarnation is a paradox, a mystery – God made one of us in the life of Jesus Christ, connecting heaven and earth. These acts of worship are incarnational: they speak of the divine, but from a perspective that is earthed, rooted and grounded in human lived experience. They are incarnational, too, because they invite us to be fully involved, participating and creating the worship, opening ourselves to allow the word to become flesh in us. Incarnational worship resists the false separation of secular and spiritual, and recognizes that we are whole people, body, mind and spirit. Wor-ship has often engaged our minds, but incarnational worship seeks to involve our heart and gut as well!

At their heart, these resources are an invitation to experience silence, in a shared contemplative space. It is easy for our worship to pile words upon words, barely drawing breath in our talking at God! The real transformative encounter comes when we stop talking and allow space for reflection and listening, both to our own inner voice, and to the still small voice of God. There is so little silence in our noise-packed, information-crowded, activity-paced lives; so these moments can be an oasis of calm in a frenetic world, and can allow us to discern what is really going on in our lives, connecting us with ourselves and with God.

Creative prayers for incarnational worship centre on an encounter with the living God that can change our perceptions and our actions. Each act of worship is intended to open the possibility of change in us, for us to be different as a result of our encounter with God. This is not worship for its own sake, or as religious entertainment, but worship that expands our horizons, as we connect with the living God and with our topsy-turvy world, in all its pain and possibility. It can be transformational, if we risk opening our hearts and lives to be changed by it.

We are all apprentices, life-long learners, and as Christians, followers of Jesus, that is especially true. There is a long tradition of using Lent to take up some form of learning, reading a book, attending a Lent discussion group or course of study. This is rooted in the practice of preparing people for baptism and confirmation during the forty days of Lent, then for the catechumens to come to profess their faith on Easter Day. In a powerful service at midnight on Easter Eve in Coventry Cathedral, these apprentices are brought up out of the 'tomb' of the old ruined cathedral, and into the light of the Easter fire and to the heart of the new building. Apprenticeship carries a connotation of hands-on learning, of applied experience, of practical knowledge. It calls us to grow in a faith that begins with Jesus inviting us to 'come and see'.

The liturgies for Lent offer material for five weeks, starting with Ash Wednesday. They explore traditional themes, of self-examination, temptation and repentance, but with a contemporary connection. They look at our deepest motivations, alongside those of Jesus being tempted in the desert. For Mothering Sunday they explore the insights of Lady Julian of Norwich who could see God as both Mother and Father. The two alternative Stations of the Cross provide material for those with traditional Stations, and for many churches who are interested to explore the newer biblically-based stations.

Holy Week offers a unique opportunity for people to grow in faith. In busy lives many struggle to make space for time with God. These liturgies can be a framework for people to be involved in planning and leading worship. They include radical prayer and action for equality, an opportunity for the laying on of hands for healing and wholeness as well as the more familiar themes of the last supper and the crucifixion. The week gives scope for the slow building up of a visual focus, added to each day, or for the learning of new music, or for trying new kinds of worship that are very different to the usual Sunday service. They could be used as the heart of a retreat in daily life, where apprentices can journey together with Jesus through the days of his passion.

But apprentices can also be eyewitnesses! Not just those who saw the risen Jesus in the flesh, but us, who bear witness to the reality of resurrection life breaking through the little deaths of our own daily lives. We are called to bear witness, to dare to speak of our experiences, of our faith. We believe, not just because of a story long ago and far away, but because that story keeps on breaking into our world, here and now!

The Easter season starts in darkness. Holy Saturday offers an opportunity to focus on grief and loss, and to invite those who have been bereaved in the past year to recognize how hard it is to move on. Easter Day is all about learning to recognize Jesus in new ways, and to see the life that breaks through again and again. We are called to a culture of encounter, of taking time to be open to one another, to listen deeply, and to offer radical hospitality, that we might come to meet Jesus in the face of neighbour and stranger. To be credible eyewitnesses we will need to face our own fears and doubts, and to find a new confidence with our faith, to break out of the habitual armour of our public selves.

The season finishes with the Ascension and a challenge to go global in our vision! We often limit the possibility of what God can do with us by being too narrow and parochial, so we are invited to share the breadth of what God dreams for the world.

These acts of worship may be used by individuals, small groups or in larger settings as frameworks for silence and reflection. They have been used in church services, in quiet days, retreats, and at the end of small group discussions.

Planning and preparation

It is helpful to invite people to participate in preparing and in leading worship. It can be good to invite a group of people to come together to plan and to prepare for the service. A range of voices and faces leading worship can encourage people to identify more readily with the liturgy.

Context

The liturgies are intended to help people to reflect deeply on their personal faith, so time given to arranging an intimate setting will be well spent. Seating, lighting, shape and ambience of the room will all be important. Attention to posture and stillness will allow people to enter into the worship more fully. Even large church buildings can be made to feel more intimate with the careful use of lighting.

Visual focus

To worship God as whole people, body, mind and spirit, it can be helpful to have a visual focus, to create 'stations' in different places, or gradually to build up a place of encounter. Leaders can involve other members of the team in creating a strong visual focus, using a wide range of materials, and objects from the natural world, projected images, art and colour.

Creating a service sheet/PowerPoint presentation

The liturgies in this book are set out for the worship leader, with full notes for running the service, reflections and often the full bible passage. This is not the form that would be used in a service sheet or PowerPoint presentation where you would want to show a running order, and words of prayers but probably not print all of the reflections.

Pace

The liturgy is intended to be spacious, taken slowly and with pauses to allow people to reflect deeply on their experience. It is good to hear a variety of voices, so it may be possible to invite people to participate in reading different sections.

Silence

Silence is the key to the whole liturgy, but the leader may need to gauge how much silence a particular group can cope with. If people are completely unused to silence, it may feel uncomfortable at first, so it is essential to introduce the silence, and say how long the silence will last to help people to know what is going to happen. Some people will need a question to take with them into the silence, something to think about; others may be comfortable with a word of scripture, such as 'Be still and know that I am God', or the Jesus prayer, 'Lord Jesus Christ, Son of God, have mercy on me', or perhaps a phrase related to the theme. As the leader it is important that you are not afraid of the silence, and that you don't 'panic' into ending it early!

Responses

The responses are in bold type, and there are opportunities where these may be said or sung, or replaced with a chant or chorus, from Taizé or Iona or elsewhere.

Hymns, songs and chants

Throughout the book I have given suggestions for possible hymns, songs and chants. Most worship leaders will want to choose their own music to suit the local context, but these are offered as an option. Among the suggestions there are traditional hymns, worship songs and chants from Taizé and Iona. For those who do not have access to musicians who could play live music, it is usually possible to find recorded versions of these on-line that can be played.

Music

The use of music in the times of reflection is intended to offer yet another 'way in' to the silence. Music speaks to another part of our selves. We have found that less familiar music can add to the creative experience for people, taking them into unfamiliar places! Pieces by James MacMillan, Karl Jenkins, Arvo Pärt, Erkki-Sven Tuur, John Tavener, Gyorgy Ligeti, as well as more ancient music by Byrd, Palestrina, Hildegard of Bingen, Tallis, have all been good. Music from Taizé and Iona can give a reflective feel too. Just one thing to watch for: be aware that music with words can sometimes be a diversion, with the words getting in the way for some people. There are web links in the resources section for all the music suggested. If you are fortunate enough to have musicians who could play live music that is even better!

Endings

It is important to have a proper ending for a service: the final prayer will often be the signal for this, and will give permission for people to leave. In some settings, if there is scope after the liturgy, it can be good to play further music and allow people time to continue to be still while others leave quietly.

LENT

Dust and Ashes

Living mindfully on Ash Wednesday

Introduction

To prepare for this service you will need to set up two places of focus. The first place is a large metal dish with a candle flame at the centre where people can burn slips of paper; you can use ordinary paper, or obtain some magician's 'flash' paper that disappears in flame. The second focus is a place for the imposition of ashes, where people can kneel, sit or stand (as they are able) to receive the ashes and immediately afterwards the laying on of hands for healing and wholeness. Ashes may be produced by burning palm crosses and mixing them with a little water or olive oil.

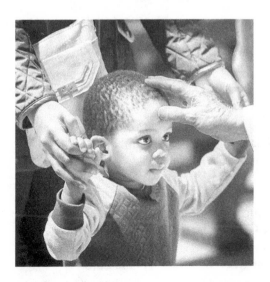

Gathering Music – *as people gather, to set the scene –*
suggestion

De Profundis, Antonio Salieri

Welcome

Welcome to this service at the beginning of Lent as we journey
with Jesus through the forty days and nights in the wilderness.
Lent is a time of reflection, self-examination and change. It's a
time to bring to God the parts of ourselves that need to change, to
let go of destructive patterns and memories, and to move on with
lighter tread. The ashes we receive in this service are symbols of
our sorrow and our mortality: we receive them gladly, as they can
lead to change and to healing. The laying on of hands for wholeness and healing remind us that God will not allow sorrow and
mortality to be the last word, that we are forgiven, and set free to
live life to the full.

Hymn/Song/Chant – *suggestions*

We rise again from ashes, Tom Conry

Empty broken here I stand, Nick Haigh; Anita Haigh

Forty days and forty nights, George Hunt Smyttan

Kyrie Eleison, Taizé Community

Responses

Seek the Lord while he may be found,
call upon him while he is near;
let the wicked forsake their way,
and the unrighteous their thoughts;
let them return to the Lord, that he may have mercy on them,
and to our God, for he will abundantly pardon.
For my thoughts are not your thoughts,
nor are your ways my ways, says the Lord.
For as the heavens are higher than the earth,

so are my ways higher than your ways
and my thoughts than your thoughts.
Isaiah 55.6–9

Opening Prayer

Wilderness God,
as we begin this journey through Lent
help us to bring the whole of ourselves
into the mystery of your presence.
Your thoughts are not our thoughts,
for you are beyond our imagination!
Your ways are not our ways,
for we have lost the path of love.
We come to you now in our weakness and vulnerability,
to find in you our healing and wholeness.
Meet us now in this place and time
and be our guide as we find the path of your love again.
Amen.

Psalm

Out of the depths I cry to you, O Lord.
Lord, hear my voice!
Let your ears be attentive
to the voice of my supplications!
If you, O Lord, should mark iniquities,
Lord, who could stand?
But there is forgiveness with you,
so that you may be revered.
I wait for the Lord, my soul waits,
and in his word I hope;
my soul waits for the Lord
more than those who watch for the morning,
more than those who watch for the morning.
O Israel, hope in the Lord!
For with the Lord there is steadfast love,
and with him is great power to redeem.

It is he who will redeem Israel
from all its iniquities.
Glory to the Father and to the Son and to the Holy Spirit
As it was in the beginning is now and shall be for ever. Amen.
Psalm 130

Reading – *Isaiah 55.10–end*

*In this reading, God promises that where we have known thorns
and briars he will bring fruitfulness*

For as the rain and the snow come down from heaven,
and do not return there until they have watered the earth,
making it bring forth and sprout,
giving seed to the sower and bread to the eater,
so shall my word be that goes out from my mouth;
it shall not return to me empty,
but it shall accomplish that which I purpose,
and succeed in the thing for which I sent it.
For you shall go out in joy,
and be led back in peace;
the mountains and the hills before you
shall burst into song,
and all the trees of the field shall clap their hands.
Instead of the thorn shall come up the cypress;
instead of the briar shall come up the myrtle;
and it shall be to the Lord for a memorial,
for an everlasting sign that shall not be cut off.

Hymn/Song/Chant – *suggestions*

God forgave my sin in Jesus' name, Carol Owens

Give thanks with a grateful heart, Henry Smith

Lord, I lift your name on high, Rick Founds

Listen, Lord, John L. Bell (WGRG)

Reading – *Mark 1.9–13*

In those days Jesus came from Nazareth of Galilee and was baptized by John in the Jordan. And just as he was coming up out of the water, he saw the heavens torn apart and the Spirit descending like a dove on him. And a voice came from heaven, 'You are my Son, the Beloved; with you I am well pleased.'
And the Spirit immediately drove him out into the wilderness. He was in the wilderness forty days, tempted by Satan; and he was with the wild beasts; and the angels waited on him.

Living Word of God,
Live in our lives today.

Reflection

Out of the Depths
Ash Wednesday is a time to inhabit the deepest part of ourselves, perhaps to face up to some of the things that we have buried deep, some of the memories and experiences that have hurt us, and we have not been able to face, perhaps to look at some parts of ourselves that are hidden, the deeper longings and hopes that we have not been able to bring to the surface for all sorts of reasons, maybe because of the busyness of our lives. Out of the depths we cry to God, and find that God is here in the depths with us. As we dare to enter the wilderness of our deepest selves we take hold of the hand that steadies and guides us. And in facing some of these deep hurts and vulnerabilities, we find our deeper self can begin to surface. Isaiah's words of prophecy are hopeful, they speak of the word of God accomplishing his purpose, bringing life and fruitfulness in place of dryness and thorns. In Mark's account of Jesus' baptism and temptation there is a similar coming together of struggle and affirmation. The words from heaven affirm the deepest part of who Jesus is: 'You are my Son, the Beloved; with you I am well pleased.' And they lead him into a struggle at the very depths of his being.

We share a few minutes of quiet reflection where we write onto slips of paper the 'briars and thorns', those things that need addressing in our lives, the regrets, sorrows, weaknesses, sins, memories and hurts that we would leave behind us. Then we move to the imposition of ashes to express this struggle, and to receive the laying on of hands for healing and wholeness.

Shared Silence *(three to four minutes of quiet music) – suggestion*

Nocturne in E Minor Op 72 No 1, Chopin

Action

The same music is played again as we come to burn our strips of paper in the flame, letting go of the things we have written. We then move to the place of Ashes, where we receive the imposition of ashes on our forehead, or on our palms; and the laying on of hands for healing and wholeness.

Imposition of Ashes *– using the words*

Dust you are and to dust you shall return.

Laying on of Hands *– using the words*

You are my child, my beloved, know my healing love for you.

Hymn/Song/Chant *– suggestions*

There is a redeemer, Melody Green

Bring your best to their worst, John L. Bell (WGRG)

Bless the Lord, O my soul, Taizé Community

Prayers of Recognition

We leave with God our thorns and briars,
all that we have let go of today,
and we trust God to receive them and to hold them.
For we shall go out in joy,
and be led forth in peace.

We leave with God the voices of negativity,
all that continues to undermine us,
And we trust God to receive them and to hold them.
For we shall go out in joy,
and be led forth in peace.

We offer to God our hidden selves,
all that we hope and dream for,
and we trust God to receive them and to hold them.
For we shall go out in joy,
and be led forth in peace.

We listen for God's word of affirmation,
that we are God's children, loved and called,
and we dare to trust in that voice above all others.
For we shall go out in joy,
and be led forth in peace.

Prayers of Intercession

For all who are struggling today
with the depths of stress, depression or other mental illness.
Out of the depths,
We cry to you, O God.

For all who are facing their mortality today
with illness or bad news,
Out of the depths,
We cry to you, O God.

For all who are bereaved today,
knowing that we are dust, that we may know we are also
  much loved.
Out of the depths,
We cry to you, O God.

For all who make resolutions today,
who long for change in their lives, and for resolve to keep them.
Out of the depths,
We cry to you, O God.

Collect

God of our deepest selves,
as we walk with Jesus in the wilderness,
as we face our fears and doubts,
as we leave behind all that has weighed us down,
may we tread with lightened step,
through the forty days of Lent,
knowing that we are dust,
and to dust we shall return,
but will come to Easter filled with joy,
knowing that we are loved
and meant for life with you for ever.
Amen.

Blessing

God who loves us to our very depths.
Jesus who saves us from our very worst.
Spirit who moves us to become our true selves.
Bless us now and through all the days of Lent
and bring us to life in your love.
Amen.

Hymn/Song/Chant – *suggestions*

Gather us in, Marty Haugan

Dear Lord and Father, John Greenleaf Whittier

Hungry – Falling on my knees, Kathryn Scott

Who am I?
Provider, celebrity, hero, or servant

Temptations for today

Introduction

This liturgy could be used as a pilgrimage between three prayer stations with people moving between them, or people could remain still with a single place of focus that is added to for each stage of the service. With larger numbers it may be better to use the liturgy in its separate sections over a number of occasions. It could be used at a Lent Study Group, and spread through the weeks of Lent. It could also work as the 'ministry of the word' to be followed by a Eucharist in an ordinary Sunday service.

You will need to prepare each of the stations, as follows:

Provider – *Have three large smooth stones, and three similarly sized loaves of bread or rolls as a central focus. Each person will also need a smaller stone to add to make a cairn. Among the loaves place slips of paper with short phrases of Jesus' teaching. Some examples might include: 'I came that they may have life, and have it abundantly' (John 10.10); 'My grace is sufficient for you, for power is made perfect in weakness' (2 Corinthians 12.9); 'but those who wait for the Lord shall renew their strength, they shall mount up with wings like eagles, they shall run and not be weary, they shall walk and not faint' (Isaiah 40.31); 'God is our refuge and strength, a very present help in trouble' (Psalm 46.1); 'but store up for yourselves treasures in heaven, where neither moth nor rust consumes and where thieves do not break in and steal' (Matthew 6.20).*

Celebrity – *Have a 'Jenga' set of building blocks, part built into a tower, with enough additional bricks for each person to add to the tower.*

Hero – *Have pictures of powerful world leaders, past and present – Stalin, Putin, Churchill, Hitler, Trump, etc. – mounted on card to stiffen them. You will need enough for each person to choose one, though you can have duplicates! These may be arranged on a black cloth on a low table at the front of the gathering.*

Gathering Music – *suggestion*

The deer's cry, Arvo Pärt

Welcome

In Lent we remember Jesus taking forty days and nights in the wilderness, at the very beginning of his public ministry, to wrestle with the temptations of who he was called to be. In this time together we will explore those same temptations, wrestle with the same questions Jesus faced, and reflect on who *we* are called to

be as we follow him. Lent is traditionally a time when people prepared for baptism and confirmation. It is a time of learning and
reflection, a time of apprenticeship!

Provider

Hymn/Song/Chant – *suggestions*

We lift you up, Brenton Bryan

I heard the voice of Jesus say, H. Bonar

Bless the Lord, John L. Bell (WGRG)

Responses

Unless the Lord builds the house,
Those who build it labour in vain.
Unless the Lord guards the city,
The guard keeps watch in vain.
It is in vain that you rise up early,
And go late to rest.
Eating the bread of anxious toil,
For he gives sleep to his beloved.
Psalm 127.1–2

Prayer

Lord Jesus,
You faced your own temptation in the wilderness,
help us now as we face ours.
Be with us as we set aside this time,
As we step away from our busyness, concerns and worries.
Help us to look honestly at our own lives and motivations,
And with you, to turn our back on all that distorts us.
May we learn to live like you,
by every word that comes from the mouth of God.
Amen.

Reading – *Matthew 4.1–4*

Then Jesus was led up by the Spirit into the wilderness to be tempted by the devil. He fasted forty days and forty nights, and afterwards he was famished. The tempter came and said to him, 'If you are the Son of God, command these stones to become loaves of bread.' But he answered, 'It is written, "One does not live by bread alone, but by every word that comes from the mouth of God."'

Living Word of God,
Live in our lives today.

Reflection

'The last act is the greatest treason. To do the right deed for the wrong reason', T. S. Eliot.

Each of the temptations for Jesus tested his motivation. Each offered a different way of doing the right thing for the wrong reason. In this first temptation Jesus is hungry, famished: he has fasted for so long. If he were the son of God, he could use his power to turn stones to bread, he could use his life to feed the hungry, to be the great provider. In the feeding of the multitudes we see how this could have been and Jesus realizes that people are beginning to follow him for a full belly, not for that deeper nourishment of the spirit. You sometimes see people today who thrive on meeting other people's needs, they reverse the Beatles theme 'All you need is love' to make it 'All I love is need!' There is a temptation for the church to become the great provider, and to have people grateful and dependant on us. Jesus' reply to the tempter remind us that the deeper hunger in us is not satisfied by bread but by the living word of God. In the quietness we reflect on our relationships, and those who rely on us, and our motivation when we give or when we help others. Are we tempted to become the great provider?

Silence *(about three minutes)*

Action

We are invited to come to lay our stone to form a cairn, to symbolize the laying down of any motivations or drives that are destructive or self-serving.
We then pick a sliver of paper from among the bread, and hear God's word for us.

During this action we sing a chant or song – suggestions

In love you summon, in love I follow, John L. Bell (WGRG)

Eat this bread, Taizé Community

Bread of heaven on thee we feed, Josiah Condor

Prayers of Recognition

We think of our deepest motivations and drives,
including those which are self-serving, which we have laid down.
(Silence)

Living Word of God,
Feed us.

We bring to you our deepest needs and hungers.
We hear your word for us, and hold it in our hearts.
(Silence)

Living Word of God,
Feed us.

We bring to you our relationships,
all who we depend on,
all who depend on us.
Help us to give and receive
freely and whole-heartedly,
recognizing and encouraging
mutuality and healthy interdependence.
(Silence)

Living Word of God,
Feed us.

Responses

I am the bread of life.
Whoever comes to me will never be hungry,
Whoever believes in me
will never be thirsty.
John 6.35

Celebrity

Hymn/Song/Chant – *suggestions*

Morning glory, H. Vanstone

Our Lord, you were sent, Carolyn Winfrey Gillette

Broken vessels, Joel Houston and Jonas Myrin

Lo I am with you! John L. Bell (WGRG)

Responses

We ponder your steadfast love, O God,
In the midst of your temple.
Your name, O God, like your praise,
Reaches to the ends of the earth.
Your right hand is filled with victory.
Let Mount Zion be glad.
Psalm 48.9–11

Prayer

Lord Jesus,
Often un-seen, un-noticed, un-regarded,
Your touch brings healing,
Your word brings hope,

You stand at the door and knock.
You wait for our invitation.
Be with us now as we walk with you
In the way that leads to life.
Amen.

Reading – *Matthew 4.5–7*

Then the devil took him to the holy city and placed him on the pinnacle of the temple, saying to him, 'If you are the Son of God, throw yourself down; for it is written, "He will command his angels concerning you", and "on their hands they will bear you up, so that you will not dash your foot against a stone."' Jesus said to him, 'Again it is written, "Do not put the Lord your God to the test."'

Living Word of God,
Live in our lives today.

Reflection

Everything in our culture pushes us to climb the ladder of success to reach the dizzy heights, like Jesus on the pinnacle of the Temple! We are tempted by advertisements and the lives we see in the media to strive for an ever higher standard of living. We enjoy the culture of celebrity, of famous people who have achieved these heights. Even more, we love to see them fall! One of the other possible ways for Jesus to live his life was to become a celebrity, to impress people with his powers, to gather a huge following, to show off! Instead he chose the opposite way, to climb down the ladder of success, to work unseen. In Mark's Gospel in particular, we see him asking people not to tell others what he has done for them. In this time of quietness we think of our ambitions, the ladders we are climbing, the pinnacles we wish we could ascend, and our own temptations to put God to the test.

Silence *(about three minutes)*

Action

We are invited to add a piece to the 'Jenga' tower, to symbolize the ambitions and desires we hold in our hearts, the pinnacles we wish to ascend. As we do so, we ask God to help us to see through them, to test them for their true worth.

During this action we sing a chant or song – suggestions

Listen, Lord, John L. Bell (WGRG)

Magnificat, Taizé Community

As the deer longs for the water, Martin Nystrom

Prayers of Recognition

As we think of the ambitions and desires of our hearts,
help us to choose the ones that lead to life,
to walk with Jesus in the ways of humble service.
(Silence)

Angels of light,
Guard us in all our ways.

As we think of our celebrity culture,
help us to value those who are often un-noticed,
to walk with Jesus in honouring the lost and least.
(Silence)

Angels of light,
Guard us in all our ways.

As we think of the ways we long for recognition,
help us to know the inner confidence
of being loved for who we are.
(Silence)

Angels of light,
Guard us in all our ways.

Responses

When they call to me,
I will answer them.
I will be with them in trouble.
I will rescue them and honour them.
Psalm 91.15

Hero

Hymn/Song/Chant – *suggestions*

All hail the power of Jesus' name, Edward Perronet

Greater, Chris Tomlin

Adoramus te domine, Taizé Community

Heaven and earth, John L. Bell (WGRG)

Responses

All the nations you have made
Shall come and bow down before you, O Lord.
And shall glorify your name,
For you are great and do wondrous things.
You alone are God.
You alone are God.
Psalm 86.9–10

Prayer

Lord Jesus,
You laid aside the ways of power and might.
You emptied yourself, taking the form of a servant.
You show God's power made perfect in our human weakness.
Help us to recognize where we are wielding power
and to walk with you in the ways of gentleness and peace.
Amen.

Again, the devil took him to a very high mountain and showed him all the kingdoms of the world and their splendour; and he said to him, 'All these I will give you, if you will fall down and worship me.' Jesus said to him, 'Away with you, Satan! For it is written, "Worship the Lord your God, and serve only him."'

Then the devil left him, and suddenly angels came and waited on him.

Living Word of God,
Live in our lives today.

Reflection

Another possible path for Jesus to take was that of political or military power. Many in Israel hoped for a Messiah who would come to liberate them from the Roman occupation. He could have chosen to use his personal following to incite an uprising, and attempted to change things by force. In our time, we too are tempted to solve things with power. The use of force in recent years has proved problematic for the leaders of the nations: it seems to complicate rather than to resolve things. On a personal level, we have to face our own issues with power. At work and in relationships, people can wield power inappropriately, by bullying, or manipulating others. The same temptations apply, both globally and personally. In this time of silence we think of our own power, or sense of powerlessness. We ask for wisdom in the way we use our power.

Silence *(about three minutes)*

Action

We are invited to pick up a picture of a world leader, past or present, and in pairs to discuss how they used the power that they exercised. Was it for good or ill, for the common good or for personal gain?

Prayers of Recognition

We bring to God the leaders of the nations,
all who have power over other people,
and we pray for them.
(Silence)

Worship the Lord your God,
And serve only him.

We bring to God our own use of power,
all who we have power over,
and we pray for them.
(Silence)

Worship the Lord your God,
And serve only him.

We bring to God our own sense of powerlessness or vulnerability,
the places where we feel unable to move or change,
and we pray for them.
(Silence)

Worship the Lord your God,
And serve only him.

Responses

Praise the Lord, all you nations,
Extol him, all you peoples.
For great is his steadfast love toward us,
And the faithfulness of the Lord endures forever.
Praise the Lord.
Praise the Lord.
Psalm 117.2

Hymn/Song/Chant – *suggestions*

Meekness and majesty, Graham Kendrick

Give thanks with a grateful heart, Henry Smith

Laudate omnes gentes, John L. Bell (WGRG)

Not by might, Ben Cantelon

Blessing

God who meets us in the wilderness,
give us grace to see through the subterfuge
of competing desires and ambitions.
Jesus who emptied himself of all but love,
who stands with us in temptation,
strengthen us to walk with you.
Holy Spirit, present with us now,
purify our motives,
empower our living,
and open our hearts to receive your blessing.
Amen.

Wilderness

Desolation and consolation
in the desert places

Introduction

This simple liturgy could be used each week of Lent alongside a Lent study group, or a Lent lunch, and is based on the structure of the Daily Examen, devised four hundred years ago by St Ignatius of Loyola. He developed a way of prayerful reflection, looking back over the past day, and looking forward to the next day, working with our sense of consolation and desolation when reflecting on particular events in our lives.

Gathering Music – *suggestion*

Voice in the Wilderness for Cello and Orchestra (1936),
Ernest Bloch II Poco lento

Becoming Aware of God's Presence

Welcome

In the busyness of our lives we often find it hard to pray and to reflect. We can be absorbed in meeting the varied demands of home and family, work or searching for work, caring for children or elderly relatives, commitments and obligations: all this can crowd in on our lives, leaving us no space to breathe. And when we do have a moment, the clamour of entertainment, social media, and television can fill our leisure time. The Gospels tell us that Jesus sought out lonely desert places away from the hustle and bustle, that he stayed in wilderness places, to be open to God. Lent can offer us a time to 'fast' from some of our busyness, to carve out some intentional space, to find our own desert, wilderness place. In this time together, we will share that desert place, and give time to listen deeply for the heartbeat of God in our lives. We begin with a time of stillness and silence. As thoughts of those competing demands of our life come to us, we gently recognize them and lay them down. It may help to repeat a simple phrase 'Be still and know that I am God', as we lay down each stray thought, each preoccupation.

Silence *(for about 3 minutes)*

Opening Prayer

God you are present here,
whether we recognize you or not,
whether we acknowledge you or not.
You are present,
within us, between us and around us.

Your Holy Spirit is holding us in being
and the energy of your love suffuses the universe.
May we become aware of your presence in this space and time,
aware of your heartbeat of love,
aware of your longing for us.
Speak to us through stillness and silence,
through music and word.
Give us grace to listen and to hear you
in the depths of our selves.
Amen.

Responses

O Lord, my heart is not lifted up,
my eyes are not raised too high;
I do not occupy myself with things too great and too marvellous
    for me.
But I have calmed and quieted my soul,
like a weaned child with its mother;
My soul within me is like a weaned child.
O Israel, hope in the Lord
from this time on and for evermore.
Psalm 131

Hymn/Song/Chant – *suggestions*

Jesus, your spirit in us is a wellspring, Taizé Community

Be still for the presence of the Lord, David J. Evans

Wonder and stare, John L. Bell (WGRG)

Jesus, be the centre, Michael Frye

Reviewing the Week with Gratitude

Reading – *Philippians 4.4–9*

Rejoice in the Lord always; again I will say, Rejoice. Let your gentleness be known to everyone. The Lord is near. Do not worry about anything, but in everything by prayer and supplication with thanksgiving let your requests be made known to God. And the peace of God, which surpasses all understanding, will guard your hearts and your minds in Christ Jesus.

Finally, beloved, whatever is true, whatever is honourable, whatever is just, whatever is pure, whatever is pleasing, whatever is commendable, if there is any excellence and if there is anything worthy of praise, think about these things. Keep on doing the things that you have learned and received and heard and seen in me, and the God of peace will be with you.

Living Word of God,
Live in our lives today.

Reflection

Paul encourages us to 'Rejoice in the Lord always', so we give time to reflect on the events of this past week, reviewing the week with gratitude for all that has been, giving thanks for the gift of life itself. Perhaps surprisingly, even the tough memories can be a cause of rejoicing because they can be a place from which to grow. In our mind's eye we allow the events of each day to scroll through our minds, good memories and tough ones too – conversations, conflicts, disappointments in ourselves and in others, high and low points. For each one, as we pay attention to our emotions, does it bring a sense of consolation or desolation, do we feel better or worse as we remember it? You may like to take a piece of paper, for this reflection, making a private note of key events under the two headings of 'Consolation' and 'Desolation', depending on the positive or negative feelings associated with the memory of the event.

Pavan, William Byrd

Choosing One Memory and Praying with It

Response

When I thought, 'My foot is slipping',
your steadfast love, O Lord, held me up.
When the cares of my heart are many,
your consolations cheer my soul.
Psalm 94.18–19

Reflection

Of all the memories that we have held, there may have been one that evoked a particularly strong reaction, a powerful emotional response. It might be a positive one, something that has been deeply resonant with your life and faith. It might be more negative, something that has left you feeling desolate, ashamed or hurt. Whichever you choose, hold one memory and the feelings that it has awoken, as the focus for this next time of prayer.

Prayers of Recognition

Abiding God,
you know the best in us,
you know the worst in us,
Your love for us remains
steadfast, unchanging, and resolute.
Be our rock, our refuge
as we dare to look at our deepest selves.
(Silence)

When the cares of my heart are many,
your consolations cheer my soul.

God of change,
you know what we can be,
you know what needs to change in us.
Your call to us remains
constant, open and dynamic.
Be our guide and helper now as we hold this memory.
(Silence)

When the cares of my heart are many,
your consolations cheer my soul.

God of transformation,
you know we find it hard to change,
you know we easily revert to old patterns, old ways.
Hold us now in our longing to grow,
renew in us your vision of what we might become.
(Silence)

When the cares of my heart are many,
your consolations cheer my soul.

Looking Towards Tomorrow

Hymn/Song/Chant – *suggestions*

O Lord, hear my prayer, Taizé Community

Listen, Lord, John L. Bell (WGRG)
Father, hear the prayer we offer, Maria Willis

Prayers of Intercession

From the heart of our inner journey, we look outwards to pray
for others. We focus on St Paul's words, holding them for all who
are in need of prayer today. 'The Lord is near. Do not worry
about anything, but in everything by prayer and supplication with
thanksgiving let your requests be made known to God.'
Philippians 4.5

As Jesus knew wilderness solitude,
we pray for those who face life on their own,
any who are lonely, abandoned, bereaved.
(Silence)

The Lord is near,
Let your requests be made known to God.

As Jesus wrestled with temptations,
we pray for those who struggle in the wilderness of addiction,
any who are uncomfortable in the place they find themselves and
   who long to be free.
(Silence)

The Lord is near,
Let your requests be made known to God.

As Jesus made some key choices about his life,
we pray for those who are facing big decisions today,
including any who are unsure of the way forward.
(Silence)

The Lord is near,
Let your requests be made known to God.

As Jesus found his true vocation in the wilderness,
we pray for those who are listening for God's call,
any who have yet to find their true self.
(Silence)

The Lord is near,
Let your requests be made known to God.

In the quietness
we make our own deepest prayer
to the God who always hears us.
(Silence)

The Lord is near,
Let your requests be made known to God.

Hymn/Song/Chant – *suggestions*

The peace of the Lord be with you, Guatemalan traditional, trans. Christine Carson

Peace to you, Graham Kendrick

Dona nobis pacem, Taizé Community

Make me a channel of your peace, Sebastian Temple

Blessing

God of our becoming,
true, honourable, just and pure;
Ground of our being,
pleasing, commendable, excellent, worthy;
Heart of our longing,
bringing change and expanding our horizons of love,
Bless us now,
Father, Son and Holy Spirit.
Amen.

Mothering God

All Shall Be Well

Introduction

On the fourth Sunday of Lent it is traditional to celebrate Mother-
ing Sunday, and churches will often share a gift of flowers for all
women attending church. This day can be an intensely painful
experience for some, including those who long for children but are
unable to have them. Churches often celebrate Mothering Sunday
by focusing on Mary the mother of Jesus as a pattern for our
human parenting. Another way is to reflect on the Mothering of
God, inspired by the insights of Julian of Norwich, a fourteenth-
century anchoress and mystic, who addressed God as both Father
and Mother.

You will need a table with enough flowers and greenery, wire or tape, to enable everyone to make a posy of flowers; a place for these completed posies to be offered; and a place for the lighting of candles of remembrance.

Gathering Music – *suggestion*

Lament for Jerusalem, John Tavener

Welcome

Today we celebrate Mothering Sunday by reflecting on the mothering of God. A fourteenth-century woman called Julian of Norwich was both anchoress and mystic, and she saw God as both mother and father. We are going to join in the Mothering Sunday tradition of giving posies of flowers in a different way this morning, both making and sharing the posies together. We will also share an opportunity to give thanks for our own mothers, and to light a candle of remembrance for those who have died.

Hymn/Song/Chant – *suggestions*

She sits like a bird, brooding on the waters, John L. Bell (WGRG)

Come now is the time to worship, Brian Doerkson

Meekness and majesty, Graham Kendrick

Ubi caritas, Taizé Community

Responses

O Lord, my heart is not lifted up,
my eyes are not raised too high;
I do not occupy myself with things too great
and too marvellous for me.
But I have calmed and quieted my soul,
like a weaned child with its mother;
my soul is like the weaned child that is with me.

O Israel, hope in the Lord
from this time on and for evermore.
Psalm 131

Prayer

Mothering God,
embrace us in your fierce love,
enfold us in your protective care,
calm our anxious worrying,
quieten our teeming minds,
still us, body, mind and spirit,
to rest in you,
like a weaned child.
Amen.

Reading – *Hosea 11.1–4*

When Israel was a child, I loved him,
 and out of Egypt I called my son.
The more I called them, the more they went from me;
they kept sacrificing to the Baals, and offering incense to idols.
Yet it was I who taught Ephraim to walk, I took them up in
 my arms;
 but they did not know that I healed them.
I led them with cords of human kindness, with bands of love.
I was to them like those who lift infants to their cheeks.
 I bent down to them and fed them.

Living Word of God,
Live in our lives today.

Reading

As truly as God is our Father, so truly is God our Mother.
I understand three ways of contemplating motherhood in God.
The first is the foundation of our nature's creation; the second is

his taking of our nature, where the motherhood of grace begins; the third is the motherhood at work . . . and it is all one love.
From 'Showings' by Julian of Norwich

Hymn/Song/Chant – *suggestions*

Mothering God, Jean Janzen (based on Julian of Norwich), tune John L. Bell (WGRG)

Lord, you have my heart, Lenny Leblanc

Adoramus te domine, Taizé Community

Be still for the presence of the Lord, David J. Evans

Gospel Reading – *Matthew 23.37–9*

'Jerusalem, Jerusalem, the city that kills the prophets and stones those who are sent to it! How often have I desired to gather your children together as a hen gathers her brood under her wings, and you were not willing! See, your house is left to you, desolate. For I tell you, you will not see me again until you say, "Blessed is the one who comes in the name of the Lord."'

Living Word of God,
Live in our lives today.

Reflection

I wonder if you remember the moving documentary about Rio Ferdinand the footballer and his life caring for his children after the death of his wife. It was called 'Being mum and dad' and for a macho celebrity was incredibly revealing about what it would take for him to be mum as well as dad. It touched some of the same themes we are exploring today. God is so often seen in male terms, most of us grew up thinking that God is masculine and are most familiar calling God our Father. But to do so is to miss half of the picture. The Book of Genesis tells us that we are created male and female in the image of God. So what are the attributes of a mothering God? What gifts did Rio need to develop or access to be a good mum as well as a dad to his children? What would it mean for each of us to reflect the mothering of God in our lives? Male and female, we are complete when we can embrace the whole of ourselves.

Silence *(about three minutes)*

Action

As the music begins, we choose some flowers and greenery from the table to make a small posy of flowers, giving thanks for our own mothers, and for the gift of mothering in each of us. We place these ready for distribution to everyone as an offering of the whole of ourselves, and a thanksgiving for the whole community's gift of mothering.

Music – *suggestion*

Lakme: Flower duet *(five minutes)*, Leo Delibes

Prayers of Recognition

God of all creativity, beauty and grace,
when we feel stressed, bent out of shape and unable to change,
restore us to our true self.
(Silence)

As a mother comforts her child,
So I will comfort you.
Isaiah 66.13

God of all loving, vulnerability and care,
when we feel unloved, unlovely, and uncared for,
embrace us with your healing grace.
(Silence)

As a mother comforts her child,
So I will comfort you.

God of all believing, longing and transforming,
when we are filled with self-doubt or distrust and when we
    feel hopeless,
help us to see ourselves through your eyes.
(Silence)

As a mother comforts her child,
So I will comfort you.

Mothering God,
as you have brought us to birth,
fed us and nurtured us with your love,
seen in us the possibilities and potential
of who we might become,
so may your gift of life-giving, horizon-stretching mothering
overflow in us
and touch those around us with your love.
Amen.

Hymn/Song/Chant – *suggestions*

Now let us sing, traditional, adapted by John L. Bell (WGRG)

Open the eyes of my heart, Michael W. Smith

O the love of my Lord, Estelle White

Prayers of Intercession

*Julian of Norwich was known for her confidence in God that 'All
shall be well, and all shall be well and all manner of things shall
be well.'*
For those who are parenting children,
those who feel overwhelmed,
those who struggle to cope,
(Silence)

All shall be well, and all shall be well,
and all manner of thing shall be well.
Julian of Norwich

For parents who are struggling to stay together,
those who are separated, alone, unhappy,
for adoptive parents and step parents,
for those seeking to build a new relationship,
(Silence)

All shall be well, and all shall be well,
and all manner of thing shall be well.

For parents who struggle to feed their family,
those who live with conflict, violence and fear,
those who have had to flee their homes,
(Silence)

All shall be well, and all shall be well,
and all manner of thing shall be well.

For all children,
both those who know in their bones that they are loved
and those who are living with uncertainty and insecurity,
(Silence)

All shall be well, and all shall be well,
and all manner of thing shall be well.

For our own mothers,
and for all who mothered us,
(Silence)

All shall be well, and all shall be well,
and all manner of thing shall be well.

Sharing of Flowers and Lighting of Candles

During this final song, women, men and children all come forward to receive flowers. For those whose mothers have died, there is an opportunity to light a candle of remembrance and thanksgiving.

Hymn/Song/Chant – *suggestions*

Now thank we all our God, Martin Rinkart

Thank you, Ben Fielding, Reuben Morgan

Mayenziwe – Your will be done, traditional South African

Blessing

Mother, Father God,
bringing the universe to birth,
nurturing and feeding
healing and reconciling,
bless us now,
men and women,
in all our mothering.
Amen.

Compassion

Stations of the Cross
The gift of tears in a desperate world

Introduction

Visitors to the Holy Land have found that it can be so powerful to walk in the footsteps of Jesus, especially on the Via Dolorosa, the Way of the Cross, in Jerusalem. This profound pilgrimage has been celebrated in many ordinary churches, both Catholic and Protestant, through the Stations of the Cross. Two alternative sets of reflections follow; firstly, the traditional stations that have been developed over the last 500 years; and then a more contemporary set of stations, more biblically rooted.

If the service is to take place in a church with Stations of the Cross already in place, you may want to use those stations, otherwise you may like to obtain a set of posters (see Resources) or to connect with a local artist, or a group from church, to create Stations of your own. Either way, you will want to give thought to how to move around the Stations safely and with thought to people with disabilities. Where people cannot manage to stand for long, or to move easily, Stations can be projected onto a screen, with people remaining seated.

These Stations can be led by one person, but it is much more powerful to have a different person leading each Station.

You will need the following to prepare for actions during the Stations:

1   *A large rough wooden cross to be carried between stations: it needs to be strong enough to be dropped.*
2   *A rough cloth to be passed between people and held for a moment.*
3   *Three nails to be hammered into the cross.*
4   *A large sheet to be ripped from top to bottom.*

Chants

The singing of a chant signals the move to the next Station
Use the same chant throughout the pilgrimage, choosing one of these suggestions

Don't be afraid, my love is stronger, John L. Bell (WGRG)

Goodness is stronger than evil, Desmond Tutu, John L. Bell (WGRG)

We will lay our burden down, John L. Bell (WGRG)

Bless the Lord my soul, Taizé Community

Traditional Stations of the Cross

Gathering Music – *suggestion*

St John Passion, Arvo Pärt

Introduction

Today we will walk in the footsteps of Jesus, in the way of the cross; we open ourselves to share in his suffering, his arrest and trial, his torture and death. This is a profound and moving experience and, if we allow it, a transforming one. Walking with Jesus in his passion can help us to recognize that we walk in his footsteps as we live through our own trials, our own painful memories. The journey may even bring us to tears. Tears, in all their vulnerability, are a profound gift of God: they can express sorrow and pain and they can equally express joy and thankfulness. Tears often come at a moment of release or realization, as a sacrament, an outward and visible sign of an inward and spiritual grace. Before he entered Jerusalem, Jesus stood weeping at the plight of the people. His compassion, his tears, moved him towards the way of the cross.

Reading – *Luke 19.41–4*

As he came near and saw the city, he wept over it, saying, 'If you, even you, had only recognized on this day the things that make for peace! But now they are hidden from your eyes. Indeed, the days will come upon you, when your enemies will set up ramparts around you and surround you, and hem you in on every side. They will crush you to the ground, you and your children within you, and they will not leave within you one

stone upon another; because you did not recognize the time of
your visitation from God.'

Prayer

Compassionate God,
as we walk with Jesus
in the way of the cross
touch us deeply.
If we encounter tears,
may we know them as your gift,
blessing us as we offer you
our own deepest struggles and pain.
May your passionate love
for each of us
and for this world
release in us the energy to live through all things,
offering the most painful places to you,
trusting in your love which changes and transforms even the
    toughest experiences.
As we offer this pilgrimage,
we offer ourselves;
walk with us now, we pray.
Amen.

We turn to the first station.

1 Pilate condemns Jesus to die

Leader

The first station – Pilate condemns Jesus to die.

Responses

We adore you, O Christ, and we bless you.
By your holy cross, you have redeemed the world.

Reading – *Luke 23.20–5*

Pilate, wanting to release Jesus, addressed them again; but they kept shouting, 'Crucify, crucify him!' A third time he said to them, 'Why, what evil has he done? I have found in him no ground for the sentence of death; I will therefore have him flogged and then release him.' But they kept urgently demanding with loud shouts that he should be crucified; and their voices prevailed. So Pilate gave his verdict that their demand should be granted. He released the man they asked for, the one who had been put in prison for insurrection and murder, and he handed Jesus over as they wished.

Reflection

Fear is at the heart of this act of injustice. For Pilate, it's the fear that he will lose control of the crowd if he doesn't go along with them. For the religious authorities, it's the fear that Jesus will undermine their traditions and their monopoly on God. And for the fickle crowd, who were so recently crying Hosanna to welcome Jesus, what's the fear for them? Crowds take on a dynamic of their own, but they are made up of people like us, with all our personal agendas – fears about looking foolish, of being excluded, of being disappointed. We condemn people today, building them up one moment, toppling them the next. Pilate could find no grounds, no evidence, no reason, but all these mean nothing when we want blood.

Silence *(about one minute)*

When have I gone along with the crowd?
When have I seen injustice and done nothing?

Prayer

Jesus, you were condemned,
but you do not condemn us.
We shed tears of shame.
No one stood up for you,

no one defended you;
your innocence was clear,
but our fear won the day.
Have mercy upon us,
and give us grace to speak out
in the face to injustice today.
Jesus, by your cross,
save us and help us, we pray.
Amen.

Chant – *As we move to the next station*

2 Jesus accepts his cross

Leader

The second station – Jesus accepts his cross.

Responses

We adore you, O Christ, and we bless you.
By your holy cross, you have redeemed the world.

Reading – *John 19.17*

So they took Jesus; and carrying the cross by himself, he went out to what is called The Place of the Skull, which in Hebrew is called Golgotha.

Reflection

In the face of the crowd's fears and passions, Jesus hardly speaks, he appears almost passive. Jesus does not respond, does not defend himself or hit back, he accepts the cross. This is not weakness or compliance, it is much deeper than that. Jesus had said, 'turn the other cheek' and now, when it really counts, he shows us how to live that out. When someone hurts us we can choose not to retaliate, not to hurt back. This is a powerful passivity, accepting and enduring, when something cannot be changed.

Silence *(about one minute)*

What am I facing that cannot be changed?
Where do I need to be able to endure?

Jesus, seeing your suffering
we shed tears of sorrow.
You didn't deserve the cross,
you didn't hurt anyone,
you turned the other cheek
and absorbed all that was thrown at you,
choosing not to pass it on,
but our cruelty won the day.
Have mercy upon us
when we throw things at others,
showing us a different way;
and give us grace to endure
when things are thrown at us.
Jesus, by your cross,
save us and help us, we pray.
Amen.

3 Jesus falls for the first time

Leader

The third station – Jesus falls for the first time.

Action

We hear the clatter of the cross as it falls to the ground.

Responses

We adore you, O Christ, and we bless you.
By your holy cross, you have redeemed the world.

Reading – *Psalm 38.17–20*

For I am ready to fall, and my pain is ever with me. I confess
my iniquity; I am sorry for my sin.
Those who are my foes without cause are mighty, and many
are those who hate me wrongfully.
Those who render me evil for good are my adversaries because
I follow after good.

Reflection

The weight of the cross was too much to bear alone and tradition has it that Jesus fell under its weight. An innocent man,
condemned to a criminal's death, he was carrying a burden that
was not his own. Human weakness and injustice had played its
part; human cruelty and inhumanity had devised the path. The
cross represents the weight of human sin and hate, carried by a
man who showed only love and goodness. The decisions we make
can add to the burdens that others have to bear: our trading with
poorer nations, our demand for cheap products, our shirking of

responsibility, our passing on the blame, our shaming of others, can all add to that weight.

Silence *(about one minute)*

How honest can I be about my own failings and sin?
How does my living add to others' burdens?

Prayer

Jesus, in the face of your humanity
we shed tears of failure:
we admit that our choices
add to the weight you bear.
Beyond all human enduring,
you stumbled and fell,
you took our worst and absorbed it.
Have mercy upon us
and give us grace, when we stumble,
to stand again.
Jesus, by your cross,
save us and help us, we pray.
Amen.

Chant – *As we move to the next station*

4 Jesus greets his mother, Mary

Leader

The fourth station – Jesus meets his mother, Mary.

Responses

We adore you, O Christ, and we bless you.
By your holy cross, you have redeemed the world.

Reading – *John 19.26–7*

When Jesus saw his mother and the disciple whom he loved standing beside her, he said to his mother, 'Woman, here is your son.' Then he said to the disciple, 'Here is your mother.' And from that hour the disciple took her into his own home.

Reflection

We know that Mary stayed close throughout the day of the crucifixion and John's Gospel records Jesus calling to her, asking John to care for her and she for him, and creating new bonds of family between them. Parents who have had to watch their children suffer and die know what this encounter will have been like. It is so much out of the natural order. The incredible intimacy of bearing and suckling a child can create a bond that goes to the core of who we are as parents and children. Our children, our parents, bring tears of joy and of sorrow at different times.

Silence *(about one minute)*

What would I say to my child, my parent, if I could?

Prayer

Jesus, beloved son,
we shed tears of love,
for the deepest bonds of relationship,
for our parents,
for our children,
for our own losses and separation,
for key relationships torn apart by violence or distrust.
Have mercy upon us
and give us grace in our deepest relationships.
Jesus, by your cross,
save us and help us, we pray.
Amen.

Chant – *As we move to the next station*

5 Simon helps carry the cross

Leader

The fifth station – Simon helps carry the cross.

Responses

We adore you, O Christ, and we bless you.
By your holy cross, you have redeemed the world.

Reading – *Mark 15.21*

> They compelled a passer-by, who was coming in from the country, to carry his cross; it was Simon of Cyrene, the father of Alexander and Rufus.

Reflection

So much of our life isn't chosen. Events just happen to us, unexpected, unlooked for, sometimes unwanted. Why me? Simon would have every excuse to say, 'Why me?' Jesus was nothing to him, a stranger: why should he have to carry the cross? Sometimes we are thrown into such situations and we can choose how to respond. Our willingness to share a burden, to give time, to go out of our way, can transform someone else's situation. Jesus said that whenever we give even a cup of water to someone in need, we do so to him. One day we may need to rely on the kindness of strangers, when we are in need.

Silence *(about one minute)*

Have I ever asked, 'Why me?'
Am I sharing someone else's burden?
Have I been helped by a stranger?

Prayer

Jesus, helped by Simon,
we shed tears of thankfulness
for the kindness of strangers,
helping in time of need,
acknowledging those who help us bear the weight we carry.
Have mercy upon us
when we fail to recognize you
in the faces of those we meet;
and give us grace to see you
in the face of friend and stranger.
Jesus, by your cross,
save us and help us, we pray.
Amen.

Chant – *As we move to the next station*

6 Veronica wipes the face of Jesus

Leader

The sixth station – Veronica wipes the face of Jesus.

Action

A rough cloth is passed from person to person, held for a moment by each, as we remember this act of compassion.

Responses

We adore you, O Christ, and we bless you.
By your holy cross, you have redeemed the world.

Reading – *Isaiah 53.2–3*

For he grew up before him like a young plant, and like a root out of dry ground; he had no form or majesty that we should look at him, nothing in his appearance that we should desire him. He was despised and rejected by others; a man of suffering and acquainted with infirmity; and as one from whom others hide their faces he was despised, and we held him of no account.

Reflection

Sometimes the suffering we see in the world around us can be completely overwhelming. We can feel inadequate to the task of responding: 'What can I do that would make a difference?' The legend of Veronica stepping out from the crowd to wipe the spit and mud from the face of Jesus may not be found in the Bible, but it is to be found in the spirit of Jesus' teaching. The Good Samaritan who stops and cares in small practical ways cannot deal single-handedly with the problem of crime on the road, but his care makes all the difference to the man who fell among thieves. Veronica's gesture is brave: why get involved? In her small act of compassion, Veronica for a moment restores human dignity to Jesus.

Silence *(about one minute)*

When have I felt overwhelmed and powerless to help?
How can I do one small thing to restore someone's human dignity?

Prayer

Jesus, touched by Veronica,
we shed tears of joy,
for the courage of those who reach out, restoring human dignity,
making even a small difference.
Have mercy upon us
when we miss the opportunity
to share a human gesture that connects.
Give us the compassion

to reach out
and give us grace to care.
Jesus, by your cross,
save us and help us, we pray.
Amen.

Chant – *As we move to the next station*

7 Jesus falls for the second time

Leader

The seventh station – Jesus falls for the second time.

Responses

We adore you, O Christ, and we bless you.
By your holy cross, you have redeemed the world.

Reading – *Matthew 23.37–9*

'Jerusalem, Jerusalem, the city that kills the prophets and stones those who are sent to it! How often have I desired to gather your children together as a hen gathers her brood under her wings, and you were not willing! See, your house is left to you, desolate. For I tell you, you will not see me again until you say, "Blessed is the one who comes in the name of the Lord."'

Reflection

The agony of Jesus falling under the weight of the cross is a powerful reminder of his humanity, his vulnerability, his weakness. Sometimes we mistakenly think of Jesus as being superhuman, all knowing, all powerful, worker of signs and wonders. However, it is the humanity of Jesus that can reach out and connect with our own vulnerable, fragile lives. We know what it is like to keep on falling: sometimes we can't believe how many knocks we have to face in life. Sometimes we go on repeating destructive and harmful patterns, despite all our best intentions.

Silence *(about one minute)*

Where do I keep falling?
What damaging patterns do I keep repeating?

Prayer

Jesus, seeing your humanity
we shed tears of recognition
for the weakness and vulnerability
you share with us.
When we keep falling,
in all the damaging patterns of our own lives,
Help us to find you,
as we acknowledge our own weakness.
Have mercy upon us
when we are at our weakest
and give us grace to stand again.
Jesus, by your cross,
save us and help us, we pray.
Amen.

Chant – *As we move to the next station*

8 Jesus meets the women of Jerusalem

Leader

The eighth station – Jesus meets the women of Jerusalem.

Responses

We adore you, O Christ, and we bless you.
By your holy cross, you have redeemed the world.

Reading – *Luke 23.27–8*

A great number of the people followed him, and among them were women who were beating their breasts and wailing for him. But Jesus turned to them and said, 'Daughters of Jerusalem, do not weep for me, but weep for yourselves and for your children.'

Reflection

Do you sometimes find yourself weeping in sad films? It is almost as if it is easier to express grief for a person who is distant to us. We sometimes find it hard to express our true feelings for our own losses: we keep ourselves busy to avoid being overwhelmed. The women of Jerusalem were caught up in this kind of public grief, and when Jesus spoke to them it was to direct them to 'weep for yourselves and for your children'.

Silence *(about one minute)*

What losses have I known?
Have I been able to grieve?

Prayer

Jesus, who brings us home to ourselves,
help us to face our own losses,
to weep for our own pain,
to walk through the valley of the shadow of death,
and not to fear.
Have mercy upon us
when we fail to acknowledge our own weakness,
and give us grace to grieve.
Help us, with the women of Jerusalem,
to weep for ourselves,
and through tears to know your healing love.
Jesus, by your cross,
save us and help us we pray.
Amen.

9 Jesus falls for the third time

Leader

The ninth station – Jesus falls for the third time.

Responses

We adore you, O Christ, and we bless you.
By your holy cross, you have redeemed the world.

Reading – *Psalm 42.3–5*

My tears have been my food day and night, while people say to me continually, 'Where is your God?' These things I remember, as I pour out my soul: how I went with the throng, and led them in procession to the house of God, with glad shouts and songs of thanksgiving, a multitude keeping festival. Why are you cast down, O my soul, and why are you disquieted within me? Hope in God; for I shall again praise him, my help.

Reflection

'Where is your God?' Where is God in such cruelty and suffering? It's a question that each of us face for ourselves, for our loved ones and for our world, when the worst happens and things just keep on going wrong. 'God, why can't you stop this?' 'My tears have been my food day and night.' Can there be any more tears? So many give up on faith in the face of such suffering: even Jesus cried out from the cross, 'Why have you forsaken me?'

Silence *(about one minute)*

We hold our own moments of desolation in the silence
We hold the desperate situations we face in the silence

Prayer

Jesus, in your desolation,
when tears become our food day and night,
you draw near to us.
In your weakness, in your falling,
you meet us.
Have mercy upon us
when we are helpless in the face of grief and suffering
and give us grace to cling to you,
through the darkest times.
Jesus, by your cross,
save us and help us, we pray.
Amen.

Chant – *As we move to the next station*

10 Jesus is stripped of his clothes

Leader

The tenth station – Jesus is stripped of his clothes.

Responses

We adore you, O Christ, and we bless you.
By your holy cross, you have redeemed the world.

Reading – *John 19.23–4*

When the soldiers had crucified Jesus, they took his clothes and divided them into four parts, one for each soldier. They also took his tunic; now the tunic was seamless, woven in one piece from the top. So they said to one another, 'Let us not tear it, but cast lots for it to see who will get it.'

Reflection

The final degradation was to strip Jesus naked and display him to the people. Clothes protect us from the environment, they keep us warm. Clothes protect our modesty, our privacy, and most of us are glad to cover our bodies in public. Clothes express so much of who we are, they are an extension of our personality. In stripping Jesus, they hoped to degrade and dishonour him, to humiliate and diminish him. What they could not strip away was God's glory in human form, the word made flesh, the love that would stop at nothing.

Silence *(about one minute)*

When have I been humiliated?
When have I felt at my most exposed?

Prayer

Jesus, in your nakedness,
when all is stripped away,
we see your true glory,
clothed with love
that will stop at nothing.
Have mercy upon us
when we believe that loss and humiliation
will have the final word;
give us grace to know ourselves,
our bodies, as glorious in your sight.
Jesus, by your cross,
save us and help us, we pray.
Amen.

Chant – *As we move to the next station*

11 Jesus is nailed to the cross

Leader

The eleventh station – Jesus is nailed to the cross.

Responses

We adore you, O Christ, and we bless you.
By your holy cross, you have redeemed the world.

Reading – *Luke 23.32–4*

Two others also, who were criminals, were led away to be put to death with him. When they came to the place that is called The Skull, they crucified Jesus there with the criminals, one on his right and one on his left. Then Jesus said, 'Father, forgive them; for they do not know what they are doing.'

Action

Nails are driven into the cross.

Reflection

Human beings are capable of such savagery! To take a nail and drive it through skin and bone, flesh and blood, knowing the agony it will cause: how can a person do that? How can we become so distorted? The gas chambers and killing fields of the world are testimony that this savagery is only just under the surface. Often it evokes a cycle of revenge and retribution that continues through generations. The only response that can stop this vicious circle is to be heard from Jesus: 'Father, forgive them, for they do not know what they are doing.'

Silence *(about one minute)*

Who has hurt me?

Who have I found hard to forgive?
Can this be my prayer? 'Father, forgive them, for they do not
know what they are doing.'

Prayer

Jesus, in your agony,
as nails are driven through your hands and feet,
we weep with sorrow at our savagery.
We hold the memory of our own bitter pain
in the stream of your forgiveness.
Have mercy upon us
when we hurt you and others:
help us to face the hurt honestly and,
from our hearts, to ask for forgiveness.
When we are hurt, give us grace to forgive,
as we have been forgiven.
Jesus, by your cross,
save us and help us, we pray.
Amen.

Chant – *As we move to the next station*

12 Jesus dies on the cross

Leader

The twelfth station – Jesus dies on the cross.

Responses

We adore you, O Christ, and we bless you.
By your holy cross, you have redeemed the world.

Reading – *Mark 15.33–7*

When it was noon, darkness came over the whole land until three in the afternoon. At three o'clock Jesus cried out with a loud voice, 'Eloi, Eloi, lema sabachthani?', which means 'My God, my God, why have you forsaken me?' When some of the bystanders heard it, they said, 'Listen, he is calling for Elijah.' And someone ran, filled a sponge with sour wine, put it on a stick, and gave it to him to drink, saying, 'Wait, let us see whether Elijah will come to take him down.' Then Jesus gave a loud cry and breathed his last.

Action

A large sheet is torn from top to bottom.

Reflection

Death is the great unknown, the last enemy, the thing we don't mention! We prefer to talk of 'passing on' or 'falling asleep': we dare not speak death's name and yet it comes to every one of us. This was a bitter death, an agonizing death: Jesus felt abandoned by God, was misunderstood by the bystanders and cried out in agony. Yet what he did changed everything. The ultimate enemy is defeated, death has become the gate of glory. Everything changes – and the curtain in the temple is torn from top to bottom!

A thousand years later his disciple, Francis of Assisi, was able to welcome death, recognizing that Jesus' death changes death for each and every one of us: 'and thou, most kind and gentle death, waiting to hush our latest breath, thou leadest home the child of God, and Christ our Lord the way hath trod'.

Silence *(about one minute)*

Can death become a friend and not an enemy?

Prayer

Jesus, in your death
you shared the fear and pain and desolation
of our human condition.
You weep with us.
We bring to you our own fear,
the hard deaths we have known,
the grief and pain and loss.
Have mercy upon us
and give us grace to face death
without fear.
Jesus, by your cross,
save us and help us, we pray.
Amen.

Chant – *As we move to the next station*

13 Jesus is taken down from the cross

Leader

The thirteenth station – Jesus is taken down from the cross.

Responses

We adore you, O Christ, and we bless you.
By your holy cross, you have redeemed the world.

Reading – *John 19.25, 31–3*

Meanwhile, standing near the cross of Jesus were his mother, and his mother's sister, Mary the wife of Clopas, and Mary Magdalene.

Since it was the day of Preparation, the Jews did not want the bodies left on the cross during the sabbath, especially because that sabbath was a day of great solemnity. So they asked Pilate to have the legs of the crucified men broken and the bodies removed. Then the soldiers came and broke the legs of the first and of the other who had been crucified with him. But when they came to Jesus and saw that he was already dead, they did not break his legs.

Reflection

The casual brutality of the soldiers is captured in the detail of this scene, breaking the legs of the crucified to tidy them away, to get the job done. But what happened next? One of the most moving images of the crucifixion is Michelangelo's The Pietà, the Pity, the moment when the body of Jesus is taken down from the cross and laid in his mother's arms. The worst has happened. The tenderness of Mary's response cannot undo the hurt, it cannot blot out the casual brutality, it cannot reverse her son's death, but it does express solidarity with all those who have seen the worst happen.

Silence *(about one minute)*

Can we meet brutality with tenderness?
When we have received the worst, can we accept reality and live
from that point?

Prayer

Jesus, in your cross we see the casual brutality of our world,
in your living and in your dying
you meet our violence with your tenderness,
our hatred with your pity.
With Mary we bring to you our hurts and disappointments,
the sword that pierces our own heart.
Have mercy upon us
when our hearts and hopes, our bodies and beliefs, are broken
and give us grace to let go into your embrace.
Jesus, by your cross,
save us and help us, we pray.
Amen.

Chant – *As we move to the next station*

14 Jesus is placed in the tomb

Leader

The fourteenth station – Jesus is placed in the tomb.

Responses

We adore you, O Christ, and we bless you.
By your holy cross, you have redeemed the world.

Reading – *Matthew 27.57–61*

When it was evening, there came a rich man from Arimathea, named Joseph, who was also a disciple of Jesus. He went to Pilate and asked for the body of Jesus; then Pilate ordered it to be given to him. So Joseph took the body and wrapped it in a clean linen cloth and laid it in his own new tomb, which he had hewn in the rock. He then rolled a great stone to the door of the tomb and went away. Mary Magdalene and the other Mary were there, sitting opposite the tomb.

Reflection

How do you make amends? When you know you have done wrong, how do you make it right? Pilate knew in his heart of hearts that Jesus was innocent: Pilate had acted out of political necessity. Joseph of Arimathea, like all of the disciples, had been helpless, unable to stop the relentless path of events. Now, both men could try to redeem the situation by acting honourably, giving Jesus the dignity of a proper burial, a clean shroud and a new tomb. We all get things wrong, but do we have the courage to try to put things right? Or we may be like the women, the Marys, who have done all that needs to be done, so that they do not need to busy themselves with action at this point: for them, they simply stay with it, they sit and wait.

Silence *(about one minute)*

Is there something that needs putting right in my life?

Prayer

Jesus, your love sets us free from past mistakes,
you show us how we can set things right.
May our tears give us clear sight
either to take the action needed to move forwards
or simply to be where we are and wait.
Give us the courage we need to

wait in your presence and to walk in your way.
Have mercy upon us
and give us grace to draw breath, simply to be there,
and, when the time is right, to take the next step.
Jesus, by your cross,
save us and help us, we pray.
Amen.

Chant – *As we move to the final gathering place*

15 The promise of the resurrection

Leader

The fifteenth station – the promise of the resurrection.

Responses

We adore you, O Christ, and we bless you.
By your holy cross, you have redeemed the world.

Reading – *Mark 8.34–5*

Jesus called the crowd with his disciples, and said to them, 'If
any want to become my followers, let them deny themselves and
take up their cross and follow me. For those who want to save
their life will lose it, and those who lose their life for my sake,
and for the sake of the gospel, will save it.'

Reflection

The way of the cross reminds us of Jesus' paradox that we have
to be prepared to let go of life to find it. Can we deny ourselves?
That is, can we set aside SELF, our ego needs, our self-absorption,
to be turned inside out, to live for others? Can we take up our
cross? That is, can we grasp the hard things that need dealing with
in our lives, can we stick in the tough places, not avoiding the

painful and uncomfortable realities of lives? Can we follow Jesus? Can we learn his way of forgiveness, reconciliation, of dying and living? The resurrection life begins today!

Silence *(about one minute)*

We commit ourselves anew to resurrection life, denying self, taking up our cross, trusting in the path through death to life, following Jesus.

We adore you, O Christ, and we bless you.
By your holy cross, you have redeemed the world.
God chose what is weak in the world to shame the strong.
We adore you, O Christ, and we bless you.
We preach Christ crucified,
the power of God and the wisdom of God.
By your holy cross, you have redeemed the world.
God forbid that I should glory,
save in the cross of our Lord Jesus Christ.
We adore you, O Christ, and we bless you.
By your holy cross, you have redeemed the world.

Hymn – *suggestions*

Morning glory, W. H. Vanstone

There is a green hill far away, Cecil Frances Alexander

When I survey the wondrous cross, Isaac Watts

In Christ alone, Keith Getty and Stuart Townend

Thank you for the cross, Graham Kendrick

Biblical Stations of the Cross

Gathering Music – *suggestion*

St John Passion, Arvo Pärt

Introduction

Today we will walk in the footsteps of Jesus, in the way of the cross. We open ourselves to share in his suffering, his arrest and trial, his torture and death. This is a profound and moving experience and, if we allow it, a transforming one. Walking with Jesus in his passion can help us to recognize that we walk in his footsteps as we live through our own trials, our own painful memories. The journey may even bring us to tears. Tears, in all their vulnerability, are a profound gift of God: they can express sorrow and pain and they can equally express joy and thankfulness. Tears often come at a moment of release or realization, as a sacrament, an outward and visible sign of an inward and spiritual grace. Before he entered Jerusalem, Jesus stood weeping at the plight of the people. His compassion, his tears, moved him towards the way of the cross.

Reading – *Luke 19.41–4*

As he came near and saw the city, he wept over it, saying, 'If you, even you, had only recognized on this day the things that make for peace! But now they are hidden from your eyes. Indeed, the days will come upon you, when your enemies will set up ramparts around you and surround you, and hem you in on every side. They will crush you to the ground, you and your children within you, and they will not leave within you one stone upon another; because you did not recognize the time of your visitation from God.'

Prayer

Compassionate God,
as we walk with Jesus
in the way of the cross
touch us deeply.
If we encounter tears,
may we know them as your gift,
blessing us as we offer you
our own deepest struggles and pain.
May your passionate love
for each of us
and for this world
release in us the energy to live through all things,
offering the most painful places to you,
trusting in your love which changes and transforms even the
   toughest experiences.
As we offer this pilgrimage,
we offer ourselves;
walk with us now, we pray.
Amen.

We turn to the first station.

1 Jesus in the Garden of Gethsemane

Leader

The first station – Jesus in the Garden of Gethsemane.

Responses

We adore you, O Christ, and we bless you.
By your holy cross, you have redeemed the world.

Reading – *Mark 14.32–6*

They went to a place called Gethsemane; and he said to his disciples, 'Sit here while I pray.' He took with him Peter and James and John, and began to be distressed and agitated. And he said to them, 'I am deeply grieved, even to death; remain here, and keep awake.' And going a little farther, he threw himself on the ground and prayed that, if it were possible, the hour might pass from him. He said, 'Abba, Father, for you all things are possible; remove this cup from me; yet, not what I want, but what you want.'

Reflection

This is Jesus at his most human: just like us, he is terrified of what the future might hold and he prays from the heart, 'Remove this cup from me.' It is the same prayer that has been repeated by people in countless situations, 'Please, not this.' Please, not cancer, not dementia, not divorce, not redundancy, not this. If we find ourselves in this place, we know he has been here before us. His honesty and example can help us to pray from the heart, acknowledging honestly how hard it feels, how strongly we resist what we can see ahead; and then daring to go one step further in trust, to hand ourselves over to God, as we say: 'Your will be done.'

Silence *(about one minute)*

What is it that I am dreading?
Can I dare to hand it over to God?

Prayer

Jesus, in Gethsemane,
your tears, your fears, your honesty
reveal your humanity.
When we are desperate,
hear our cry.

When we are fearful and alone
be with us.
Have mercy upon us
when we are overwhelmed
and give us grace to
open our hearts to you
and then to say, in trust,
'your will be done'.
Jesus, by your cross,
save us and help us, we pray.
Amen.

Chant – *As we move to the next station*

2 Jesus is betrayed by Judas

Leader

The second station – Jesus is betrayed by Judas.

Responses

We adore you, O Christ, and we bless you.
By your holy cross, you have redeemed the world.

Reading – *Mark 14.43–5*

Immediately, while he was still speaking, Judas, one of the twelve, arrived; and with him there was a crowd with swords and clubs, from the chief priests, the scribes, and the elders. Now the betrayer had given them a sign, saying, 'The one I will kiss is the man; arrest him and lead him away under guard.' So when he came, he went up to him at once and said, 'Rabbi!' and kissed him.

Reflection

It always hurts when it is someone close who betrays you. Judas was one of the twelve, one of the inner circle, trusted with the common purse. He betrays Jesus with a kiss. He uses an outward show of intimacy and friendship as the means of betrayal. When our trust is betrayed, through infidelity, dishonesty, or abuse, it can leave us deeply damaged, unable to dare to trust again. Sometimes it will be us who have betrayed another's trust, through intention or by accident, through weakness or cowardice. Either way, betrayed or betrayer, how do we go on? Is there a future for us?

Silence *(about one minute)*

When have I been betrayed?
When have I betrayed someone?

Prayer

Jesus, you always see the best in us,
the person we could become,
just as you saw the good in Judas.
When we have betrayed our best selves,
help us to face you again in honesty.
When we have been betrayed
by someone we love,
protect us from lasting harm.
Have mercy upon us
and give us grace to dare to trust again.
Jesus, by your cross,
save us and help us, we pray.
Amen.

Chant – *As we move to the next station*

3 Jesus is condemned by the Sanhedrin

Leader

The third station – Jesus is condemned by the Sanhedrin.

Responses

We adore you, O Christ, and we bless you.
By your holy cross, you have redeemed the world.

Reading – *Mark 14.55–6, 60–4*

Now the chief priests and the whole council were looking for
testimony against Jesus to put him to death; but they found
none. For many gave false testimony against him, and their
testimony did not agree.

Then the high priest stood up before them and asked Jesus,
'Have you no answer? What is it that they testify against you?'
But he was silent and did not answer. Again the high priest asked

him, 'Are you the Messiah, the Son of the Blessed One?' Jesus said, 'I am; and "you will see the Son of Man seated at the right hand of the Power", and "coming with the clouds of heaven".'

Then the high priest tore his clothes and said, 'Why do we still need witnesses? You have heard his blasphemy! What is your decision?' All of them condemned him as deserving death.

Reflection

We live in a time of fake news where it is hard to get hold of the truth. Politicians are happy to 'spin' the facts to make them fit their narrative. As Jesus was tried before the religious leaders they hoped that false witnesses would be enough to condemn him, but even their testimony didn't hang together. They didn't really need witnesses, they had already made up their minds. Prejudice is about closing your mind to the truth, choosing to see the world through your own pre-judgement. It's something we all do and it takes a determined act of will to choose to remain open to the truth. In the face of false testimony, Jesus' first response is silence. The silence increases the impact of his words when he is pressed further: he speaks the truth, but this is instantly dismissed as blasphemy.

Silence *(about one minute)*

When have I been aware of my own prejudices and their impact? When have I been in a situation where the truth was rejected out of hand?

Prayer

Jesus, help us to recognize
where we have been blinded by prejudice.
Help us to see through the subterfuge of 'fake news'
and self-interest that can mislead us.
Open our eyes to your presence
in every human face
and to truth, whenever it is spoken.

Have mercy upon us
when we distort or dismiss truth
and give us grace to look and see anew.
Jesus, by your cross,
save us and help us, we pray.
Amen.

Chant – *As we move to the next station*

4 Jesus is denied by Peter

Leader

The fourth station – Jesus is denied by Peter.

Responses

We adore you, O Christ, and we bless you.
By your holy cross, you have redeemed the world.

Reading – *Luke 22.54–62*

Then they seized him and led him away, bringing him into the
high priest's house. But Peter was following at a distance. When
they had kindled a fire in the middle of the courtyard and sat
down together, Peter sat among them. Then a servant-girl,
seeing him in the firelight, stared at him and said, 'This man also
was with him.' But he denied it, saying, 'Woman, I do not know
him.' A little later someone else, on seeing him, said, 'You also
are one of them.' But Peter said, 'Man, I am not!' Then about
an hour later still another kept insisting, 'Surely this man also
was with him; for he is a Galilean.' But Peter said, 'Man, I do
not know what you are talking about!' At that moment, while
he was still speaking, the cock crowed. The Lord turned and
looked at Peter. Then Peter remembered the word of the Lord,
how he had said to him, 'Before the cock crows today, you will
deny me three times.' And he went out and wept bitterly.

Reflection

Fear can be such a distorting emotion, it can lead us to betray our values, our conscience, our deepest selves. Peter is like many of us, a mixture of courage and weakness; he runs away when the soldiers take Jesus away, but then he follows at a distance to see what will happen. When the servants begin to recognize him, he denies he ever knew Jesus. When the soldiers came to arrest and deport Jews in Germany, or Muslims in Serbia, many good people stayed silent and did nothing; fear led them to betray themselves and their neighbours. In our more ordinary lives, there are often occasions when we don't speak out, don't own up to our faith or our failures, don't stand up for truth our speak out for what we believe. The hardest moment is when we realize the full impact of our failure, our cowardice, when the cock crows. Jesus turned and looked at Peter, and it is Jesus' look that forced him face the truth in that moment and to weep tears of regret.

Silence *(about one minute)*

When has fear led me to betray my deepest self?
When has my betrayal been found out?

Prayer

Jesus, help us to face our fears,
to recognize when we betray our deepest selves.
In those moments when our courage fails us,
where we are caught out and our betrayal is uncovered,
help us to catch the full force of your loving gaze,
giving us renewed courage to work through our regret,
to repent and be forgiven.
Have mercy upon us
and give us grace to dare to start again.
Jesus, by your cross,
save us and help us, we pray.
Amen.

5 Pilate condemns Jesus to die

Leader

The fifth station – Pilate condemns Jesus to die.

Responses

We adore you, O Christ, and we bless you.
By your holy cross, you have redeemed the world.

Reading – *Luke 23.20–5*

Pilate, wanting to release Jesus, addressed them again; but they kept shouting, 'Crucify, crucify him!' A third time he said to them, 'Why, what evil has he done? I have found in him no ground for the sentence of death; I will therefore have him flogged and then release him.' But they kept urgently demanding with loud shouts that he should be crucified; and their voices prevailed. So Pilate gave his verdict that their demand should be granted. He released the man they asked for, the one who had been put in prison for insurrection and murder, and he handed Jesus over as they wished.

Action

We wash our hands in a bowl of water, as Pilate did.

Reflection

Fear is at the heart of this act of injustice. For Pilate, it's the fear that he will lose control of the crowd if he doesn't go along with them. For the religious authorities, it's the fear that Jesus will undermine their traditions and their monopoly on God. And for the fickle crowd, who were so recently crying Hosanna to welcome Jesus, what's the fear for them? Crowds take on a dynamic of their own, but they are made up of people like us, with all our personal agendas – fears about looking foolish, of being excluded, of being disappointed. We condemn people today, building them up one moment, toppling them the next. Pilate could find no grounds, no evidence, no reason, but all these mean nothing when we want blood.

Silence *(about one minute)*

When have I gone along with the crowd?
When have I seen injustice and done nothing?

Prayer

Jesus, you were condemned,
but you do not condemn us.
We shed tears of shame.
No one stood up for you,
no one defended you;
your innocence was clear,
but our fear won the day.
Have mercy upon us,
and give us grace to speak out
in the face of injustice today.
Jesus, by your cross,
save us and help us we pray.
Amen.

Chant – *As we move to the next station*

6 Jesus is flogged and crowned with thorns

Leader

The sixth station – Jesus is flogged and crowned with thorns.

Responses

We adore you, O Christ, and we bless you.
By your holy cross, you have redeemed the world.

Reading – *John 19.1–3*

Then Pilate took Jesus and had him flogged. And the soldiers wove a crown of thorns and put it on his head, and they dressed him in a purple robe. They kept coming up to him, saying, 'Hail, King of the Jews!' and striking him on the face.

Reflection

Jesus never claimed to be a king: it was a trumped-up charge, introduced to twist the truth and undermine the threat he posed to the authorities. His presence challenges their power, so it is not enough simply to kill him: he must be humiliated and belittled, undermined and made to look foolish. Pilate has Jesus flogged; the soldiers dress him up in a crown of thorns and robe and mock him. We can see the same forces at work today in politics, the media, even the Church, when people distort and vilify their opponents. In our own small way we have done the same, whenever we have joined in with laughing at someone, or mocking them. And we may also know what it feels like to be on the receiving end of such humiliation.

Silence *(about one minute)*

When have I humiliated someone, laughed at them and mocked them?
When have I been there while someone else was humiliated, laughed at or mocked, without challenging it?

When have I been humiliated, laughed at and mocked? How did it feel?

Prayer

Jesus, you were beaten and humiliated
but you turned the other cheek,
you did not strike back.
When we have been hurt by cruel laughter,
ground us with your deep confidence.
When we see others ridiculed or humiliated,
help us to stand up for those who are vulnerable
and to challenge any abuse of power.
Have mercy upon us
when we undermine others, and show us a different way,
learning from you, our King.
Jesus, by your cross,
save us and help us, we pray.
Amen.

Chant – *As we move to the next station*

7 Jesus carries his cross

Leader

The seventh station – Jesus carries his cross.

Responses

We adore you, O Christ, and we bless you.
By your holy cross, you have redeemed the world.

Reading – *John 19.17*

So they took Jesus; and carrying the cross by himself, he went
out to what is called The Place of the Skull, which in Hebrew is
called Golgotha.

Reflection

In the face of the crowd's fears and passions, Jesus hardly speaks and seems almost passive. Jesus does not respond, does not defend himself or hit back, he accepts the cross. This is not weakness or compliance, it is much deeper than that. Jesus had said 'turn the other cheek' and now when it really counts, he shows us how to live that out. When someone hurts us we can choose not to retaliate, not to hurt back. This is a powerful passivity, accepting and enduring, when something cannot be changed.

Silence *(about one minute)*

What am I facing that cannot be changed?
Where do I need to be able to endure?

Prayer

Jesus, seeing your suffering
we shed tears of sorrow.
You didn't deserve the cross,
you didn't hurt anyone,
you turned the other cheek
and absorbed all that was thrown at you,
choosing not to pass it on,
but our cruelty won the day.
Have mercy upon us
when we throw things at others,
showing us a different way;
and give us grace to endure
when things are thrown at us.
Jesus, by your cross,
save us and help us, we pray.
Amen.

Chant – *As we move to the next station*

8 Simon helps carry the cross

Leader

The eighth station – Simon helps carry the cross.

Responses

We adore you, O Christ, and we bless you.
By your holy cross, you have redeemed the world.

Action

We hear the clatter of the cross as it falls to the ground.

Reading *– Mark 15.21*

> They compelled a passer-by, who was coming in from the country, to carry his cross; it was Simon of Cyrene, the father of Alexander and Rufus.

Reflection

So much of our life isn't chosen. Events just happen to us, un-expected, unlooked for, sometimes unwanted. Why me? Simon would have every excuse to say, 'Why me?' Jesus was nothing to him, a stranger: why should he have to carry the cross? Sometimes we are thrown into such situations and we can choose how to respond. Our willingness to share a burden, to give time, to go out of our way, can transform someone else's situation. Jesus said that whenever we give even a cup of water to someone in need, we do so to him. One day we may need to rely on the kindness of strangers, when we are in need.

Silence *(about one minute)*

Have I ever asked, 'Why me?'
Am I sharing someone else's burden?
Have I been helped by a stranger?

Prayer

Jesus, helped by Simon,
we shed tears of thankfulness,
for the kindness of strangers,
helping in time of need,
acknowledging those who help us bear the weight we carry.
Have mercy upon us
when we fail to recognize you
in the faces of those we meet;
and give us grace to see you
in the face of friend and stranger.
Jesus, by your cross,
save us and help us, we pray.
Amen.

Chant – *As we move to the next station*

9 Jesus meets the women of Jerusalem

Leader

The ninth station – Jesus meets the women of Jerusalem.

Responses

We adore you, O Christ, and we bless you.
By your holy cross, you have redeemed the world.

Reading – *Luke 23.27–8*

> A great number of the people followed him, and among them
> were women who were beating their breasts and wailing for him.
> But Jesus turned to them and said, 'Daughters of Jerusalem, do
> not weep for me, but weep for yourselves and for your children.'

Reflection

Do you sometimes find yourself weeping in sad films? It is often easier to express grief for a person who is distant to us. We sometimes find it hard to express our true feelings for our own losses: we keep ourselves busy to avoid being overwhelmed. The women of Jerusalem were caught up in this kind of public grief, and when Jesus spoke to them it was to redirect them 'weep for yourselves and for your children'.

Silence *(about one minute)*

What losses have I known?
Have I been able to grieve?

Prayer

Jesus, who brings us home to ourselves,
help us to face our own losses,
to weep for our own pain,
to walk through the valley of the shadow of death,
and not to fear.
Have mercy upon us
when we fail to acknowledge our own weakness
and give us grace to grieve.
Help us, with the women of Jerusalem,
to weep for ourselves,
and through tears to know your healing love.
Jesus, by your cross,
save us and help us, we pray.
Amen.

Chant – *As we move to the next station*

10 Jesus is crucified

Leader

The tenth station – Jesus is crucified.

Responses

We adore you, O Christ, and we bless you.
By your holy cross, you have redeemed the world.

Reading – *Luke 23.32–4*

Two others also, who were criminals, were led away to be put to death with him. When they came to the place that is called The Skull, they crucified Jesus there with the criminals, one on his right and one on his left. Then Jesus said, 'Father, forgive them; for they do not know what they are doing.'

Action

Nails are driven into the cross.

Reflection

Human beings are capable of such savagery! To take a nail and drive it through skin and bone, flesh and blood, knowing the agony it will cause: how can a person do that? How can we become so distorted? The gas chambers and killing fields of the world are testimony that this savagery is only just under the surface. Often it evokes a cycle of revenge and retribution that continues through generations. The only response that can stop this vicious circle is to be heard from Jesus: 'Father forgive them; for they do not know what they are doing.'

Silence (*about one minute*)

Who has hurt me?
Who have I found hard to forgive?
Can this be my prayer? 'Father forgive them; for they do not
know what they are doing.'

Prayer

Jesus, in your agony,
as nails are driven through your hands and feet,
we weep with sorrow at our savagery.
We hold the memory of our own bitter pain
in the stream of your forgiveness.
Have mercy upon us
when we hurt you and others:
help us to face the hurt honestly and,
from our hearts, to ask for forgiveness.
When we are hurt, give us grace to forgive,
as we have been forgiven.
Jesus, by your cross,
save us and help us, we pray.
Amen.

Chant – *As we move to the next station*

11 Jesus promises the kingdom

Leader

The eleventh station – Jesus promises the kingdom.

Responses

We adore you, O Christ, and we bless you.
By your holy cross, you have redeemed the world.

Reading – *Luke 23.39–43*

One of the criminals who were hanged there kept deriding him and saying, 'Are you not the Messiah? Save yourself and us!' But the other rebuked him, saying, 'Do you not fear God, since you are under the same sentence of condemnation? And we indeed have been condemned justly, for we are getting what we deserve for our deeds, but this man has done nothing wrong.' Then he said, 'Jesus, remember me when you come into your kingdom.' He replied, 'Truly I tell you, today you will be with me in Paradise.'

Reflection

The two thieves crucified with Jesus respond to him so differently. One is embittered, and turns his suffering into derision, preferring to taunt Jesus, echoing the mockery of the soldiers and crowds. When we are hurt, we so often hit out at others. The other thief recognizes that Jesus is different, he is an innocent man, condemned unjustly – and this provokes a different response from him. On the cross, near to death, the penitent thief asks to be remembered. This is about more than not being forgotten. Jesus hears his cry to be re-membered, put back together again, made whole, restored. When our lives go wrong; when we are broken, physically, emotionally, spiritually, we too can ask Jesus to re-member us, to put us back together again; and we can hear his promise, 'Today you will be with me in Paradise.'

Silence *(about one minute)*

When I am hurt, have I hit out at others?
What is fragmented in me, needing to be re-membered and made whole again?

Prayer

Jesus, when we are hurting,
when we are broken,
when our life seems pointless and empty,
guide us to reach out to you,
to turn away from bitterness,
to be re-membered in your love.
Have mercy upon us
and give us grace to be made whole.
Jesus, by your cross,
save us and help us, we pray.
Amen.

Chant – *As we move to the next station*

12 Jesus greets his mother, Mary

Leader

The twelfth station – Jesus greets his mother, Mary.

Responses

We adore you, O Christ, and we bless you.
By your holy cross, you have redeemed the world.

Reading – *John 19.26–7*

When Jesus saw his mother and the disciple whom he loved standing beside her, he said to his mother, 'Woman, here is your son.' Then he said to the disciple, 'Here is your mother.' And from that hour the disciple took her into his own home.

Reflection

We know that Mary stayed close throughout the day of the crucifixion and John's Gospel records Jesus calling to her, asking John to care for her and her for him, and creating new bonds of family between them. Parents who have had to watch their children suffer and die know what this encounter will have been like. It is so much out of the natural order. The incredible intimacy of bearing and suckling a child can create a bond that goes to the core of who we are as parents and children. Our children, our parents, bring tears of joy and of sorrow at different times.

Silence *(about one minute)*

What would I say to my child, my parent, if I could?

Prayer

Jesus, beloved son,
we shed tears of love,
for our deepest bonds of relationship,
for our parents,
for our children,
for our own losses and separation,
for those key relationships torn apart by violence or distrust.
When we face the worst together,
give us grace to help and support one another.
Jesus, by your cross,
save us and help us, we pray.
Amen.

Chant – *As we move to the next station*

13 Jesus dies on the cross

Leader

The thirteenth station – Jesus dies on the cross.

Responses

We adore you, O Christ, and we bless you.
By your holy cross, you have redeemed the world.

Reading – *Mark 15.33–7*

> When it was noon, darkness came over the whole land until
> three in the afternoon. At three o'clock Jesus cried out with a
> loud voice, 'Eloi, Eloi, lema sabachthani?', which means, 'My
> God, my God, why have you forsaken me?' When some of the
> bystanders heard it, they said, 'Listen, he is calling for Elijah.'
> And someone ran, filled a sponge with sour wine, put it on

a stick, and gave it to him to drink, saying, 'Wait, let us see whether Elijah will come to take him down.' Then Jesus gave a loud cry and breathed his last.

Action

A large sheet is torn from top to bottom.

Reflection

Death is the great unknown, the last enemy, the thing we don't mention! We prefer to talk of 'passing on' or 'falling asleep': we dare not speak death's name and yet it comes to every one of us. This was a bitter death, an agonizing death: Jesus felt abandoned by God, was misunderstood by the bystanders and cried out in agony. Yet what he did changed everything. The ultimate enemy is defeated, death has become the gate of glory. Everything changes – and the curtain in the temple is torn from top to bottom!

A thousand years later his disciple, Francis of Assisi, was able to welcome death, recognizing that Jesus' death changes death for each and every one of us: 'and thou, most kind and gentle death, waiting to hush our latest breath, thou leadest home the child of God, and Christ our Lord the way hath trod'.

Silence *(about one minute)*

Can death become a friend and not an enemy?

Prayer

Jesus, in your death
you shared the fear and pain and desolation
of our human condition.
You weep with us.
We bring to you our own fear,
the hard deaths we have known,
the grief and pain and loss.
Have mercy upon us

and give us grace to face death,
without fear.
Jesus, by your cross,
save us and help us, we pray.
Amen.

Chant – *As we move to the next station*

14 Jesus is placed in the tomb

Leader

The fourteenth station – Jesus is placed in the tomb.

Responses

We adore you, O Christ, and we bless you.
By your holy cross, you have redeemed the world.

Reading – *Matthew 27.57–61*

When it was evening, there came a rich man from Arimathea,
named Joseph, who was also a disciple of Jesus. He went to
Pilate and asked for the body of Jesus; then Pilate ordered it to
be given to him. So Joseph took the body and wrapped it in a
clean linen cloth and laid it in his own new tomb, which he had
hewn in the rock. He then rolled a great stone to the door of
the tomb and went away. Mary Magdalene and the other Mary
were there, sitting opposite the tomb.

Reflection

How do you make amends? When you know you have done
wrong, how do you make it right? Pilate knew in his heart of
hearts that Jesus was innocent: Pilate had acted out of political
necessity. Joseph of Arimathea, like all of the disciples, had abandoned Jesus for fear of the soldiers. Now, both men could try

to redeem the situation be acting honourably, giving Jesus the dignity of a proper burial, a clean shroud and a new tomb. We all get things wrong, but do we have the courage to try to put things right? Or we may be like the women, the Marys, who have done all that needs to be done, so that they do not need to busy themselves with action at this point: for them, they simply stay with it, they sit and wait.

Silence *(about one minute)*

Is there something that needs putting right in my life?

Prayer

Jesus, your love sets us free from past mistakes,
you show us how we can set things right.
May our tears give us clear sight
either to take the action needed to move forwards
or simply to be where we are and wait.
Give us the courage we need
to wait in your presence and to walk in your way.
Have mercy upon us
and give us grace to draw breath, simply to be there,
and, when the time is right, to take the next step.
Jesus, by your cross,
save us and help us, we pray.
Amen.

Chant – *As we move to the final gathering place*

15 The promise of the resurrection

Leader

The fifteenth station – the promise of the resurrection.

Responses

We adore you, O Christ, and we bless you.
By your holy cross, you have redeemed the world.

Reading – *Mark 8.34–5*

> Jesus called the crowd with his disciples, and said to them, 'If any want to become my followers, let them deny themselves and take up their cross and follow me. For those who want to save their life will lose it, and those who lose their life for my sake, and for the sake of the gospel, will save it.'

Reflection

The way of the cross reminds us of Jesus' paradox that we have to be prepared to let go of life to find it. Can we deny ourselves? That is, can we set aside SELF, our ego needs, our self-absorption, to be turned inside out, to live for others? Can we take up our cross? That is, can we grasp the hard things that need dealing with in our lives, can we stick in the tough places, not avoiding the painful and uncomfortable realities of our lives? Can we follow Jesus? Can we learn his way of forgiveness, reconciliation, of dying and living? The resurrection life begins today!

Silence *(about one minute)*

We commit ourselves anew to resurrection life, denying self, taking up our cross, trusting in the path through death to life, following Jesus.

Leader	We adore you, O Christ, and we bless you;
All	**by your holy cross, you have redeemed the world.**
Leader	God chose what is weak in the world to shame the strong.
All	**We adore you, O Christ, and we bless you.**
Leader	We preach Christ crucified,
	the power of God and the wisdom of God.
All	**By your holy cross, you have redeemed the world.**
Leader	God forbid that I should glory,
	save in the cross of our Lord Jesus Christ.
All	**We adore you, O Christ, and we bless you;**
	by your holy cross, you have redeemed the world.

Hymn

HOLY WEEK

Do not be afraid!

Introduction

Holy Week can be a focus for deepening faith and exploring alternative modes of worship and prayer. The days of Holy Week, from Palm Sunday to Easter Day, can be an ideal time for a retreat; but many find it hard to get away, when life is just too busy, when there are too many responsibilities and constraints. A retreat in daily life within the framework of Holy Week can be an alternative that many people can manage. It can be good to involve as many people as possible in creating and leading worship. You might like to engage a team of five–ten people each day to set the scene, to lead, to read, to pray and to provide music. The idea is for people to be able to make time each day, at home or at work, to read, reflect and pray; and also to come together for a Holy Week service day by day.

Daily life retreat

Welcome

'Do not be afraid' are the words that Jesus said so often, especially to those who were feeling lonely, excluded or vulnerable. This week we will explore some of what makes us fearful and anxious. We will walk with Jesus through the last days of his life and see how he too had to face some of these same issues. 'I will call you by your name, you are mine' is the deep affirmation that God makes for us, that we belong with Jesus, that we belong in the heart of God's love.

'Do not be afraid' is a journey of discovery as we dare to step out of the ordinary patterns of our lives, to set out on a different path. Through Holy Week, we walk with Jesus as he deals with loneliness, isolation, rejection, conflict and betrayal. Each of these will take us into the heart of the Passion, finding there deep resonances with our own experience.

Palm Sunday

Called to follow
Laying down our cloaks, taking up our cross

Hymn/Song/Chant – *suggestions*

Ride on, ride on in majesty, Henry Hart Milman

All glory, laud and honour, St Theodulph of Orleans, trans. John Neale

Come, People of the Risen King, Stuart Townend

Come all you people (Uyai Mose), Alexander Gondo and John L. Bell (WGRG)

Meekness and Majesty, Graham Kendrick

Opening Prayer

Jesus, you enter our life humbly
riding on a donkey,
staying on our level,
inviting our response.
Circle our hearts
centre our minds
still our bodies
be present to us now.
Amen.

Canticle

But now thus says the Lord,
he who created you, O Jacob,
he who formed you, O Israel:
Do not fear, for I have redeemed you;
I have called you by name, you are mine.
When you pass through the waters, I will be with you;
and through the rivers, they shall not overwhelm you;
when you walk through fire you shall not be burned,
and the flame shall not consume you.
For I am the Lord your God,
the Holy One of Israel, your Saviour.
I give Egypt as your ransom,
Ethiopia and Seba in exchange for you.
Because you are precious in my sight,
and honoured, and I love you.
Glory to the Father, and to the Son, and to the Holy Spirit;
as it was in the beginning, is now and shall be for ever. Amen.

Reading – *Mark 11.1–11*

When they were approaching Jerusalem, at Bethphage and
Bethany, near the Mount of Olives, he sent two of his disciples
and said to them, 'Go into the village ahead of you, and immediately as you enter it, you will find tied there a colt that has never

been ridden; untie it and bring it. If anyone says to you, "Why are you doing this?" just say this, "The Lord needs it and will send it back here immediately."' They went away and found a colt tied near a door, outside in the street. As they were untying it, some of the bystanders said to them, 'What are you doing, untying the colt?' They told them what Jesus had said; and they allowed them to take it. Then they brought the colt to Jesus and threw their cloaks on it; and he sat on it. Many people spread their cloaks on the road, and others spread leafy branches that they had cut in the fields. Then those who went ahead and those who followed were shouting,

'Hosanna! Blessed is the one who comes in the name of the Lord!

Blessed is the coming kingdom of our ancestor David!

Hosanna in the highest heaven!'

Then he entered Jerusalem and went into the temple; and when he had looked around at everything, as it was already late, he went out to Bethany with the twelve.

Living Word of God,
Live in our lives today.

Reflection

On Palm Sunday we remember Jesus entering Jerusalem to great acclaim and popularity. The people lined the streets, calling and shouting – they thought he was their liberator, their saviour. They lay down a carpet of palm branches to welcome him. But Jesus was not what they expected, he was far from the conquering hero making a triumphal entry. In their excitement, they had lost who Jesus really was, he was lost in the crowd! For he had laid aside his majesty, emptied himself of power, and entered Jerusalem as the Servant King, humble and gentle, riding on the back of a beast of burden.

Today we take up the challenge of Palm Sunday, to be like Jesus and to lay down our pride and take up our cross. Today we come to lay down our cloaks, all the things we have to protect ourselves from our fears, our layers of protection that distance us from one another and from God; we lay down too, all the layers of self-interest and hardness of heart. We lay them down, so that with empty hands and open hearts we can receive the peace and joy and love of God.

Silence

In the silence we reflect on the question; What are your 'cloaks' that you want to lay down today?

Chant

Wait for the Lord, whose day is near, Taizé Community

Prayers of Recognition

We bring to God our 'cloaks',
all our layers of protection,
the ways we keep others at a distance,
and we lay them down.
(Silence)

Wait for the Lord.
Keep watch, take heart.

We bring to God our impatience and our expectations,
our frustrations and our unhappiness,
and we lay them down.
(Silence)

Wait for the Lord.
Keep watch, take heart.

We bring to God all that we are hoping for,
longing for, all that we are waiting for,
and we hold it all in the stream of God's grace.
(Silence)

Wait for the Lord.
Keep watch, take heart.

We bring to God all that we could be,
the hidden potential,
the possibilities in our lives
and we hold it all in the stream of God's grace.
(Silence)

Wait for the Lord.
Keep watch, take heart.

Holy Spirit of God, we wait for you.
Speak to us with your still small voice.
Quieten our fears,
hold us when we are anxious,
comfort us when we are distressed.
Renew our strength,
restore our faith,
refresh our vision.
Help us to wait with you through these days of Holy Week,
to make space in our lives, to receive you.
Amen.

Intercession

We bring to God the people and situations on our hearts.

A time of open prayer, at the end of each prayer:
Lord, hear us.
Lord, graciously hear us.

Prayer

Lord Jesus, when we lose sight of you,
crowded out by our fears and anxiety,
search us out with your piercing gaze,
find us and hold us

in your undefended heart of love,
so may we lay aside our false selves,
finding that in you we are made whole.
Amen.

Hymn/Song/Chant – *suggestions*

We will lay our burden down, John L. Bell (WGRG)

From heaven you came – The Servant King, Graham Kendrick

Closing Responses

God in our longing,
strength in our waiting,
love in our fearing,
peace in our stillness,
be now among us,
Jesus our brother,
bring us your blessing,
now and always.
Amen.

Holy Monday

Called to action
Overturning tables, prayer for the nations

Introduction

To prepare for this service you will need to obtain enough foreign coins for everyone to have one. If possible have some from developing countries as well as from more familiar ones. If it is hard to get together a range of coins, it is possible to print small copies of bank notes for these countries (available on the internet). You will need to set up a table, covered with a cloth, and to spread the coins out on the table. Later when the coins have been taken, you will need a large candle to place in the middle of the table.

Gathering Music – *suggestions*

Do not be afraid, Philip Stopford

Money, Money, Money, Abba

Welcome

We don't find it easy to talk about money! We find it can evoke embarrassment, even anger in some people. It crosses the line between our public faith and our private lives. Yet Jesus often did precisely this: many of his parables and sayings speak about what we do with our money. On Holy Monday we come to reflect on our relationship with money, our money worries and what our money choices say about our relationship with God.

Hymn/Song/Chant – *suggestions*

Jesus Christ is waiting, John L. Bell (WGRG) and Graham Maule

Give thanks with a grateful heart, Henry Smith

God is the giver of all that we are, Timothy Dudley Smith

Opening Prayer

God of true value and worth,
in a world of fool's gold and counterfeit currency,
may we discern your hallmark of love,
to find our treasure in you.
Quieten our hearts and minds,
as we still our bodies,
slow our breathing,
and open ourselves to you.
Amen.

Psalm

Be gracious to me, O God, for people trample on me;
all day long foes oppress me;
My enemies trample on me all day long,
for many fight against me.
O Most High, when I am afraid,
I put my trust in you.
In God, whose word I praise, in God I trust;
I am not afraid; what can flesh do to me?
Glory to the Father, and to the Son, and to the Holy Spirit;
as it was in the beginning, is now and shall be for ever. Amen.
Psalm 56.1–4

Bible Reading – *Mark 11.15–19*

Then they came to Jerusalem. And he entered the temple and began to drive out those who were selling and those who were buying in the temple, and he overturned the tables of the money changers and the seats of those who sold doves; and he would not allow anyone to carry anything through the temple. He was teaching and saying, 'Is it not written,

"My house shall be called a house of prayer for all the nations"?

But you have made it a den of robbers.'
And when the chief priests and the scribes heard it, they kept looking for a way to kill him; for they were afraid of him, because the whole crowd was spellbound by his teaching. And when evening came, Jesus and his disciples went out of the city.

Living Word of God,
Live in our lives today.

Reflection

How many of us struggle with money worries? Jesus taught so much about money – but we can be too afraid to mention it! When Jesus came into Jerusalem, the first thing he did was to go into the temple, the most holy place of the Jewish people. He was appalled at what he found there: money-changers, who made a profit because the people had to change their money into the temple coinage to make their offerings; dealers in animals, who exploited the people's need to make sacrifices. Instead of being a place of worship, to the glory of God, the temple had become a market place, a robber's den. Instead of being a place where God's grace was available to all, the temple was being used as a way exploiting people's faith to make money at their expense. Jesus overturned their tables and drove them out of the temple.

Our fears about money can run deep. Will I have enough? Can I pay the bills? Will I be able to afford the care I need when I am older? These worries can loom large, even when there is a safety net provided by the state. And of course in many nations of the world, there is no such protection: many people earn too little to live on, struggling to feed their families today, let alone to set aside some money to provide for the future.

Jesus calls us to overturn the tables of injustice and oppression in our world. Sometimes people think of faith as a very private matter, a purely spiritual reality, but Jesus shows us that faith changes how we act – 'faith without deeds' is worthless. He is not simply prepared to go along with the status quo, in a narrow, self-interested way: he challenges injustice and inequality, coming to 'cast down the mighty from their thrones, and raise up the humble and meek'.

So we have to look outwards, in deciding how we use our money responsibly. What does it mean to have 'enough'? Beyond that, is our disposable income simply available for our own leisure activities, or can we make choices that are generous and outward-looking? When we acknowledge that our money is not 'narrowly' ours, but is held in trust from God, to be wisely and generously used, how does that change things? Money is the 'sacrament of seriousness': it is the crunch point where we choose to put our principles into practice – or not!

Response

Music suggestion (to be played quietly during this time):
Night, Ludovico Einaudi

We take a coin from the table, and identify its country of origin, and share what we know about that country with our neighbour. As we focus on money and acknowledge inequality and injustice, what practical action can we take in response? Where do we need to overturn the tables? Where do we need to take a stand? Is our church outward looking, engaged in the struggle for justice? Personally, is there a trusted place where we can be honestly accountable for the way we chose to spend our money? Is there any way that we want to change our own use of money, as we embrace the challenge to use it responsibly?

Chant – *repeated after each prayer*

Don't be afraid, John L. Bell (WGRG)

Nothing can trouble, Taizé Community

The Kingdom of God, Taizé Community

Prayers – A House of Prayer for All the Nations

We pray that this house
will be a house of prayer for all the nations.
We hold our coins now
as we think of the many different countries they represent.
Bless all the countries of the world,
rich and poor,
strong and weak
and give us the courage
to challenge and change
injustice and inequality,
both locally and globally.

Chant.

We pray for all who are constrained by debt,
living under the weight of money worries,
feeling unable to break free from the burden of the past.

Chant.

We pray for people who are hungry today
because their families cannot afford the food they need,
and for all who are struggling to pay the bills.
We pray for all who are afraid of today.

Chant.

We pray for all who fear unemployment or redundancy,
for all who are fearful that they will not have enough money
to provide for their needs going forwards.
We pray for all who are afraid for the future.

Chant.

We pray for the changing face of finance,
for credit unions and all who are offering fair terms of finance,
for all who are working to encourage good practices of money
    management,
for all who are supporting people in moving through debt
to get their finances on a firmer footing.

Chant.

O God, overturn the tables of our false values,
of our unfair trade,
our unjust systems.
Enlist us in your company of freedom,
recruit us to the cause of justice,
unfreeze our fear,
undo our indifference,
unlock our compassion,
enable our hands
to work and act and move for you.
Amen.

Action

In silence we reflect on what one thing each of us could do to overturn the tables of injustice or to use our own money more responsibly. Could we join a credit union or volunteer with a food bank, offer support to a charity or commit to buying fairly traded goods or perhaps decide to review our own income and expenditure with a trusted friend?
In silence we place the coins back on the table around a large candle as our sign of commitment to this one action. Once all the coins are placed on the table, the candle is then lit.

Act of Commitment

Not everyone who says to me, 'Lord, Lord', will enter the kingdom of heaven, but only the one who does the will of my Father in heaven.
Matthew 7.21

Lord of all nations,
overturn the tables of our hearts,
drive out all that is selfish and complacent,
that we may become a living temple for your glory.
Strengthen in us the resolve we offer today.
May we do justice,
love mercy
and walk humbly with you our God.
Amen.

The Peace

Peace in our hearts,
Peace in our homes,
Peace in our nation,
Peace in our world.
God longs for us to know peace!

The Peace of the Lord be always with you,
and also with you.

Hymn/Song/Chant – *suggestions*

Put peace into each other's hands, Fred Kaan

Break our hearts, Vicky Beeching

This is my desire, Michael W. Smith, Hillsong Worship

Heaven shall not wait, John L. Bell (WGRG) and Graham
Maule

Closing Responses

God in our working,
wisdom in our spending,
enough in our need,
generosity in our sharing,
be now among us,
Jesus our brother,
bring us your blessing,
now and always.
Amen.

Holy Tuesday

Called to forgive
Debts and debtors, perfume and tears

Introduction

For this service you will need to obtain some costly perfume, or you could use an anointing oil that can be passed from person to person. Depending on numbers you may want to have more than one bottle. This you may want to set in a central place as a focus for the worship, perhaps with an alabaster jar on a piece of richly coloured cloth.

Gathering Music – *suggestions*

Do not be afraid, Philip Stopford

Alabaster Jar, Zach Neese and Walker Beach

Welcome

Have you ever felt undervalued, or looked down on? If we are honest, we are also sometimes guilty of looking down on others, perhaps without even realizing it. We all make judgements about other people, because of their background or their reputation. Jesus himself was looked down on because he was provincial: 'Can anything good come out of Nazareth?' In so many encounters Jesus challenges and overturns our prejudice, teaching us to see people for their true worth. On Holy Tuesday we come to reflect on the way we judge and undervalue one another, recognizing how Jesus showed us a different way of relating.

Hymn/Song/Chant – *suggestions*

Do not be afraid, George Markland

My song is love unknown, Samuel Crossman

A prophet woman broke a jar, Brian Wren

Drop, drop slow tears, Phineas Fletcher

Opening Prayer

God of saints and sinners,
in a world where many are looked down on,
many are afraid of rejection,
help us to see with your non-judgemental eyes.
Quieten our hearts and minds,
as we still our bodies,
slow our breathing,
and open ourselves to you.
Amen.

Psalm

O God, you are my God, I seek you,
my soul thirsts for you; my flesh faints for you,
as in a dry and weary land where there is no water.

So I have looked upon you in the sanctuary,
beholding your power and glory.
Because your steadfast love is better than life,
my lips will praise you.
So I will bless you as long as I live;
I will lift up my hands and call on your name.
Glory to the Father, and to the Son, and to the Holy Spirit;
as it was in the beginning, is now and shall be for ever. Amen.
Psalm 63.1–4

Reading – *Mark 14.3–9*

> While he was at Bethany in the house of Simon the leper, as he sat at the table, a woman came with an alabaster jar of very costly ointment of nard, and she broke open the jar and poured the ointment on his head. But some were there who said to one another in anger, 'Why was the ointment wasted in this way? For this ointment could have been sold for more than three hundred denarii, and the money given to the poor.' And they scolded her. But Jesus said, 'Let her alone; why do you trouble her? She has performed a good service for me. For you always have the poor with you, and you can show kindness to them whenever you wish; but you will not always have me. She has done what she could; she has anointed my body beforehand for its burial. Truly I tell you, wherever the good news is proclaimed in the whole world, what she has done will be told in remembrance of her.'

Living Word of God,
Live in our lives today.

Reflection

Jesus is eating a meal with Simon the leper when a woman comes and anoints his feet with costly perfume, and onlookers are scandalized because of the costly waste. In other accounts, Simon is critical of the woman's reputation, and thinks less of Jesus because he accepts her gift. As a leper, Simon himself knew exclusion. He would have been looked down on himself; but despite the fact that he knew the pain of exclusion, Simon still choses to judge and exclude others, dividing the world up into respectable people and sinners, the sort of people you invite to supper, and those you don't! The woman is looked down on: she is judged and condemned either for being a sinner, or for being too emotional and wasteful. But Jesus stands up for her, saying, 'She will always be remembered for this.' Jesus keeps on including people that other look down on; he helps Simon to understand that we all need forgiveness, and that we can never be good enough or respectable enough to earn God's love. God's love comes as pure gift, amazing grace.

It's one of the hardest things to accept – that there is nothing that we can do to make God love us any more and there is nothing we can do to make God love us any less! God longs for us to recognize that love, and to allow that love to transform us, for us to be forgiven and healed at the very depths of our being. Like the woman with the alabaster jar, that deep healing of our past hurts often evokes both tears and an overflowing generosity that reaches out to others.

Response

Music suggestion (to be played quietly during this time):
The Goldberg Variations Aria, Bach
We keep a time of quiet for personal reflection and think about these questions:
Where are you in the story?
Are you more like Simon or the woman with the alabaster jar?
What needs forgiving in your life?
Are there tears that need to be shed?
What will change, if we can be set free?

Anointing

After a time of reflection, we anoint one another's hands with costly perfume, making the sign of the cross, and saying 'May God's love overflow in you.' The music may be continued during this time.

Prayer

Forgiving God,
you long to heal us with your touch.
Open our hearts to your gift of unconditional love.
Anoint us with the tears of your Spirit.
Wipe away the hurts and harms of our memory
that your love may overflow in us,
and through us.
Amen.

Prayers – A house of welcome for all

We pray for all who are undervalued, looked down on
    or despised
because of their nationality, colour, or religion.
(Silence)

For we are your children
made in your image and likeness.

We pray for those who are undervalued, looked down on
    or despised
because of their gender or sexuality.
(Silence)

For we are your children
made in your image and likeness.

We pray for all who are undervalued, looked down on
    or despised
because of their poverty, disability or background.
(Silence)

For we are your children
made in your image and likeness.

We pray for all who are undervalued, looked down on
 or despised
because of their past mistakes, failures or wrongdoing.
(Silence)

For we are your children
made in your image and likeness.

The Peace

Peace in our hearts,
Peace in our homes,
Peace in our nation,
Peace in our world.
God longs for us to know peace!

The Peace of the Lord be always with you,
and also with you.

Hymn/Song/Chant – *suggestions*

Put peace into each other's hands, Fred Kaan

Break our hearts, Vicky Beeching

This is my desire, Michael W. Smith, Hillsong Worship

Brother, sister let me serve you, Richard Gillard

Closing Responses

God in our touching,
generous in judgement,
welcoming all people,
seeing your image,
be now among us,
Jesus our brother,
bring us your blessing,
now and always.
Amen.

Holy Wednesday

Called to trust
Scene changers and second fiddles,
learning humility

Introduction

For this service you will need to decide how you will offer the laying on of hands for healing and wholeness. There are many different ways to arrange this. One way is to set up a square of kneelers, chairs or places for people to kneel sit or stand, with space for four leaders to stand in the middle; who can lay on hands and pray. It may be helpful to have some small cards for leaders to remind them of the words of the prayer.

Gathering Music – *suggestions*

The kiss, Joe Niemand

The Armed Man: Torches, Karl Jenkins

Welcome

In the last week of his life, Jesus had to face terrible suffering, but perhaps the hardest experience was to be betrayed by his friends. It is those who are closest to us who have the greatest capacity to hurt us. Judas is remembered for his great betrayal, but Peter and each of the disciples also betrayed Jesus in the fear of Gethsemane. On Wednesday in Holy Week we come to face up to our fears, to recognize our betrayals and to ask for healing and wholeness, to be reconciled to God, to ourselves and to one another.

Hymn/Song/Chant – *suggestions*

Kyrie Eleison, Northumbria Community

Dear Lord and Father, John Greenleaf Whittier

Emmanuel, Vicky Beeching

A king like this, Chris Tomlin

Opening Prayer

God you know the worst in us,
our fearful betrayals,
our weakness and our frailty,
yet you go on trusting us.
Quieten our hearts and minds,
as we still our bodies,
slow our breathing,
and open ourselves to you.
Amen

Psalm

It is not enemies who taunt me
I could bear that;
it is not adversaries who deal insolently with me
I could hide from them.
But it is you, my equal,

my companion, my familiar friend,
with whom I kept pleasant company;
we walked in the house of God with the throng.
Glory to the Father, and to the Son, and to the Holy Spirit;
as it was in the beginning, is now and shall be for ever. Amen.
Psalm 55.12–14

Reading – *Mark 14.10–11, 17–21*

> Then Judas Iscariot, who was one of the twelve, went to the chief priests in order to betray him to them. When they heard it, they were greatly pleased, and promised to give him money. So he began to look for an opportunity to betray him.
>
> When it was evening, he came with the twelve. And when they had taken their places and were eating, Jesus said, 'Truly I tell you, one of you will betray me, one who is eating with me.' They began to be distressed and to say to him one after another, 'Surely, not I?' He said to them, 'It is one of the twelve, one who is dipping bread into the bowl with me. For the Son of Man goes as it is written of him, but woe to that one by whom the Son of Man is betrayed! It would have been better for that one not to have been born.'

Living Word of God,
Live in our lives today.

Reflection

Have you ever been betrayed? Are you afraid of being betrayed? We think of the many ways that we can betray the trust of others; in relationships, through infidelity; in friendship when we let someone down; in business when we serve our own interests; at work when people are overlooked or treated badly.

In our Bible reading we hear of Judas' betrayal of Jesus. It is so hard to understand his motives. Was it money – the thirty pieces of silver or the money Judas was said to have taken from the common purse? Was it power – wanting to be on the winning side and not to get caught with the losers? Or did Judas feel that he would force Jesus' hand, and begin the rebellion? In the end the motives don't really matter, the betrayal happens.

Of course Judas isn't the only one who betrays Jesus. All the disciples let him down, filled with fear they run away, and Peter even denies knowing him. It is fear that is behind most of their betrayal on that fateful evening. Fear can bring out the worst in us. It can undermine our confidence, our best selves, and leave us to act in ways we deeply regret. Fear of growing older can lead to a mid-life crisis; fear of hardship can lead to a betrayal of trust; fear of losing status can lead to selfish actions.

Response

Music may be played in the background – suggestions

Kyrie Eleison, Chris Tomlin

Prayer of the Heart, John Tavener

In this time of quiet reflection we think about these questions:
Do you still hold the hurt from a time when you have been
betrayed?
What are the fears that make us betray our best selves and betray
those around us?
What are you most afraid of?

Healing and Reconciliation

A time for the laying on of hands and of prayer for healing and
    wholeness.
Those laying on hands may pray:
'Spirit of the living God, fill you, heal you and make you whole,
    in Jesus' name. **Amen.**'

Prayer

Lord Jesus, you know our deepest fears and hurts,
our darkest secrets,
our least attractive traits.
Yet you choose to trust us and to love us.
You choose to see the best that we can be.
Help us to face our hurts and fears and trust you with them.
Help us and others to inhabit the best of ourselves,
to live up to your confidence in us.
And when we do fail,
when we do betray ourselves and others,
forgive us and help us start again.
Amen.

The Peace

Peace in our hearts,
Peace in our homes,
Peace in our nation,
Peace in our world.
God longs for us to know peace!

The Peace of the Lord be always with you,
and also with you.

Hymn/Song/Chant – *suggestions*

I heard the voice of Jesus say, Horatius Bonar

My Lord, what love is this, Graham Kendrick

Closing Responses

God in our healing,
trust in face of failure,
another chance when we betray,
loving us despite everything,
be now among us,
Jesus our brother,
bring us your blessing,
now and always.
Amen.

Maundy Thursday

Called to service
Love that gets its hands dirty

Introduction

There are three distinct stages to this service, the washing of feet, the sharing of a meal, and watching in the Garden of Gethsemane. You may like to set up three different areas and move between them as the service progresses.

For the first setting, it works well for people to sit in a circle, with enough room in the middle for the washing of feet. It is helpful to ask some people in advance if they are happy for their feet to be washed. You will need a large shallow bowl, warm water and several towels.

The second setting works well with everyone sat around a table, perhaps a long thin table between the choir stalls in church. To make a memorable gathering place, time should be taken to cover and decorate the table with a tablecloth, perhaps using candles, stones and shells. Unleavened bread and wine are needed: depending on numbers, you may want to have several communion cups and plates in circulation.

For the third setting, representing the Garden of Gethsemane, you may like to set up green plants and branches to create this effect. You will also need a rough wooden cross to lie on the floor, with three large nails and a hammer.

Gathering Music – *suggestions*

Seraph II Adagio, James MacMillan

We gather in a circle facing a bowl of water and some towels

Welcome

Maundy Thursday holds so much significance for us. Jesus shows us so much of himself and calls us to follow him. In washing our feet, he calls us to his way of humble service. In breaking bread and sharing wine he calls us to discern his presence in this, and in every meal we share. In asking us to watch with him through the darkness of the night, he shows us his humanity and calls us to stand with those who suffer.

Hymn/Song/Chant – *suggestions*

> Great God your love has called us here, Brian Wren
>
> Meekness and majesty, Graham Kendrick
>
> This is the night dear friends, Latin text Peter Abelard, trans. Richard Lyman Sturch

Opening Prayer

Servant King you kneel at our feet:
show us how to serve.
Gracious Host you break and bless the bread:
show us how to share.
Suffering Friend you pour out your heart:
show us how to wait with you.
Quieten our hearts and minds,
as we still our bodies,
slow our breathing,
and open ourselves to you.
Amen.

The Washing of Feet

Psalm of Penitence

Have mercy on me, O God, according to your steadfast love;
according to your abundant mercy blot out my transgressions.
Wash me thoroughly from my iniquity, and cleanse me from
my sin.
For I know my transgressions, and my sin is ever before me.
Against you, you alone, have I sinned, and done what is evil in
your sight,
**so that you are justified in your sentence and blameless when you
pass judgement.**

Lord, have mercy
Christ, have mercy
Lord, have mercy

Create in me a clean heart, O God,
and put a new and right spirit within me.
Do not cast me away from your presence,
and do not take your Holy Spirit from me.
Restore to me the joy of your salvation,
and sustain in me a willing spirit.

Glory to the Father, and to the Son, and to the Holy Spirit;
as it was in the beginning, is now and shall be for ever. Amen.
Psalm 51.1–4, 10–12

Reading – *John 13.1–17*

Now before the festival of the Passover, Jesus knew that his hour had come to depart from this world and go to the Father. Having loved his own who were in the world, he loved them to the end. The devil had already put it into the heart of Judas son of Simon Iscariot to betray him. And during supper Jesus, knowing that the Father had given all things into his hands, and that he had come from God and was going to God, got up from the table, took off his outer robe, and tied a towel around himself. Then he poured water into a basin and began to wash the disciples' feet and to wipe them with the towel that was tied around him. He came to Simon Peter, who said to him, 'Lord, are you going to wash my feet?' Jesus answered, 'You do not know now what I am doing, but later you will understand.' Peter said to him, 'You will never wash my feet.' Jesus answered, 'Unless I wash you, you have no share with me.' Simon Peter said to him, 'Lord, not my feet only but also my hands and my head!' Jesus said to him, 'One who has bathed does not need to wash, except for the feet, but is entirely clean. And you are clean, though not all of you.' For he knew who was to betray him; for this reason he said, 'Not all of you are clean.'

After he had washed their feet, had put on his robe, and had returned to the table, he said to them, 'Do you know what I have done to you? You call me Teacher and Lord—and you are right, for that is what I am. So if I, your Lord and Teacher, have washed your feet, you also ought to wash one another's feet. For I have set you an example, that you also should do as I have done to you. Very truly, I tell you, servants are not greater than their master, nor are messengers greater than the one who sent them. If you know these things, you are blessed if you do them.'

Living Word of God,
Live in our lives today.

Foot Washing

Music is played as the foot washing takes place – suggestion
Love each other, Graham Kendrick

Prayer

Christ Jesus,
you show us your servant heart,
emptying yourself of all but love,
kneeling at our feet,
washing away all that clings.
Give us grace to kneel with you,
to bow our proud hearts,
to empty ourselves of all false status,
to serve a broken world in your name.
Amen.

Prayers of Intercession

We pray for the powerless and downtrodden,
those without status,
those who work for low or no wages.
(Silence)

Servant King,
Teach us to serve.

We pray for those who are powerful and influential,
those who govern and legislate,
those whose work is well rewarded.
(Silence)

Servant King,
Teach us to serve.

We pray for those who care and clean,
those who often go unnoticed,
but who maintain the fabric of our world.
(Silence)

Servant King,
Teach us to serve.

We pray for those who receive care,
those who live with disability, illness or injury,
who have no choice but to be dependent on others.
(Silence)

Servant King,
Teach us to serve.

We pray for those who are weighed down with shame or guilt,
those who carry a burden of painful memories,
those who grieve the loss of a loved one.
(Silence)

Servant King,
Teach us to serve.

We move to the second station, the table of the Last Supper, as we sing

Hymn/Song/Chant – *suggestions*

Now my tongue the mystery telling, trans. Edward Caswall

Morning glory, H. W. Vanstone

We walk his way, John Bell (WGRG)

Nada te turbe, Taizé Community

The Last Supper

We sit around the table

Responses

Gracious Host you break and bless the bread,
show us how to share.
Gathering your people from the ends of the earth,
show us how to welcome.
Taking the ordinary stuff of life, you fill it with meaning,
show us how to receive.

Bible Reading – *1 Corinthians 11.23–9*

For I received from the Lord what I also handed on to you, that
the Lord Jesus on the night when he was betrayed took a loaf of
bread, and when he had given thanks, he broke it and said, 'This
is my body that is for you. Do this in remembrance of me.' In the

same way he took the cup also, after supper, saying, 'This cup is the new covenant in my blood. Do this, as often as you drink it, in remembrance of me.' For as often as you eat this bread and drink the cup, you proclaim the Lord's death until he comes.

Whoever, therefore, eats the bread or drinks the cup of the Lord in an unworthy manner will be answerable for the body and blood of the Lord. Examine yourselves, and only then eat of the bread and drink of the cup. For all who eat and drink without discerning the body, eat and drink judgement against themselves.

Living Word of God,
Live in our lives today.

The Peace

That we may discern the body of Christ in this bread, wine and
    in one another,
let us first be reconciled,
forgiving and being forgiven,
making peace in Christ who is our peace.

We exchange a sign of peace with these words:
Deep peace of the Son of Peace to you.
Peace that the world cannot give.

Chant/Song

Eat this bread, drink this wine, Taizé Community
Bread is blessed and broken, John L. Bell (WGRG)
Jesus stand among us, Graham Kendrick
Bread of heaven, Josiah Conder

The authorized person gives thanks for the gifts of bread and wine:

God gives to us the fruit of the earth,
grain and grapes, bread and wine,
We offer them with thankful hearts.

Eucharistic Prayer

Creator God, source of all life,
you hallow all that you have made,
you call us to discern your presence in the cosmos,
but we often lose sight of you.
We are sometimes blind and deaf to your purposes.
We forget we are your children,
brothers and sisters in your covenant of love.

You reach for us when we fall.
You long for us to turn.
When the time was right, you came to us in Jesus,
your Word made flesh,
human face of your love.
Emptied of all power, you stoop to embrace us.

On the night of betrayal,
Jesus gathered his disciples together
to share with them a feast of future memory.
He took bread and gave you thanks.
He broke the bread and gave it to them saying
'This is my body, broken for you.
Do this to remember me.'

After supper he took a cup of wine.
Again he gave you thanks, gave it to them and said,
'Drink this, my blood of the new covenant,
shed for you and for many,
that sins may be forgiven.
Do this to remember me.'

We remember the meals he shared.
We remember the people he included.
We remember the hungry he fed.

Pour out your Holy Spirit
on these gifts of bread and wine,

that they may be for us
the body and blood of our Lord Jesus Christ.

So feed us with the bread of heaven,
the cup of your promise,
that we may live in him
and he in us,
for ever and ever.
Amen.

The Lord's Prayer

**Our Father, who art in heaven,
hallowed be thy name;
thy kingdom come;
thy will be done;
on earth as it is in heaven.
Give us this day our daily bread.
And forgive us our trespasses,
as we forgive those who trespass against us.
And lead us not into temptation,
but deliver us from evil.
For thine is the kingdom,
the power and the glory,
for ever and ever.
Amen.**

Breaking and Sharing

Wherever hearts are broken, Jesus brings healing.
Wherever lives are torn, Jesus brings wholeness.
We break this bread
To share in the body of Christ.

We share the bread and wine with the words
**Broken for you, the body of Christ.
Shed for you, the blood of Christ.**

Prayer after Communion

Bread of heaven, you feed us,
you meet our deepest needs.
Wine of the Kingdom, you quench our thirst,
you make all things new.
Bread of community, you build bridges of hope,
you make us one body.
Wine of the Spirit, you lead us forward,
you empower our living.

We keep a time of silence

Watching and Waiting

At this point, in some traditions, it is customary to strip the church of all that is beautiful to prepare for the desolation of Good Friday, as Psalm 22 is read slowly and deliberately. After this, move to the third station, the Garden of Gethsemane.

Stand around a large wooden cross that has been laid in the centre of the 'garden'

Reading – *Mark 14.32–42*

They went to a place called Gethsemane; and he said to his disciples, 'Sit here while I pray.' He took with him Peter and James and John, and began to be distressed and agitated. And he said to them, 'I am deeply grieved, even to death; remain here, and keep awake.' And going a little farther, he threw himself on the ground and prayed that, if it were possible, the hour might pass from him. He said, 'Abba, Father, for you all things are possible; remove this cup from me; yet, not what I want, but what you want.' He came and found them sleeping; and he said to Peter, 'Simon, are you asleep? Could you not keep awake one hour? Keep awake and pray that you may not come into the time of trial; the spirit indeed is willing, but the flesh is weak.' And again he went away and prayed, saying the same words.

And once more he came and found them sleeping, for their eyes were very heavy; and they did not know what to say to him. He came a third time and said to them, 'Are you still sleeping and taking your rest? Enough! The hour has come; the Son of Man is betrayed into the hands of sinners. Get up, let us be going. See, my betrayer is at hand.'

Nails are driven into the Cross

Three nails are driven into the cross to prefigure the coming crucifixion
Silence *is kept*
We are invited to keep watch with Jesus and to reflect on his inner struggles.
In some traditions, the watch is maintained until midnight.

Reflection

Jesus is alone and lonely: 'Could you not watch with me one brief hour?'

In Gethsemane Jesus dares to own his deepest feelings, to voice his deepest longing, his heartfelt desire not to go through the coming trauma and pain and death. The same words are repeated in some form whenever a person is diagnosed with cancer or some other untreatable illness: 'Take this cup away from me.' At this terrible moment, we long for reality to be different, for the miracle, for the respite, the powerful cure. It can be hard to own up to our real feelings, particularly for people of faith: we are expected to have spiritual resources to cope.

Can we be as honest and real about our feelings as Jesus, letting go of any pretence of being more able or competent than we are, letting go of any pretence of being braver or holier or better than we really are? Can we dare to voice our own fears and feelings and doubts?

Let's take into this time of reflection our own Gethsemane moments, our own fears and disappointments, and allow Jesus' honest hand to hold them.

Silence

Final Prayer

Lord Jesus,
we wait with you in the darkness,
we will watch with you now,
in this moment when you need us.
Help us to learn from your honesty,
as we own our real feelings
about the unchosen challenges in our own life.
We don't want this cup.
Why me?
Give us grace to walk through the valley,
death's shadow,
and come to the dawn of a new day
with you.
Amen.

Good Friday

Called to honest faith and doubt
In the shadow of death

Introduction

This liturgy is a service for the last hour of the cross, from 2pm to 3pm on Good Friday, though it may be used at another time. A large, rough wooden cross can be placed centrally as a visual focus, with three large nails driven into it, for Jesus' hands and feet.

Welcome

Welcome to this solemn service of the last hour. We come to be with Jesus in his hour of need, to remember his passion and death upon the cross and to reflect on the deep themes that the cross evokes in us. Today, we use the three last words of Christ recorded in St John's Gospel as the focus for our reflection and prayer.

Opening Responses

In the shadow of our suffering
is the suffering of Jesus.
In the shadow of our weakness
is the vulnerability of the Christ.
In the shadow of our pain
is the God who cried out.
We are never rejected,
we are never abandoned.

Reading – *John 19.16–25*

So they took Jesus; and carrying the cross by himself, he went out to what is called The Place of the Skull, which in Hebrew is called Golgotha. There they crucified him, and with him two others, one on either side, with Jesus between them. Pilate also had an inscription written and put on the cross. It read, 'Jesus of Nazareth, the King of the Jews.' Many of the Jews read this inscription, because the place where Jesus was crucified was near the city; and it was written in Hebrew, in Latin and in Greek. Then the chief priests of the Jews said to Pilate, 'Do not write, "The King of the Jews", but, "This man said, 'I am King of the Jews.'"' Pilate answered, 'What I have written I have written.' When the soldiers had crucified Jesus, they took his clothes and divided them into four parts, one for each soldier. They also took his tunic; now the tunic was seamless, woven in one piece from the top. So they said to one another, 'Let us not tear it, but cast lots for it to see who will get it.' This was to fulfil what the scripture says, 'They divided my clothes among themselves, and for my clothing they cast lots.' And that is what the soldiers did.

Hymn/Song/Chant – *suggestions*

There is a green hill, Cecil Francis Alexander

How deep the Father's love for us, Stuart Townend

From heaven you came, Graham Kendrick

Here I am to worship, Tim Hughes

Here is your son

Discerning interdependence
Creating new communities of care
when others have been lost

Introduction

So we come to the first of our words from the cross, words spoken by Jesus to Mary his mother and the beloved disciple, John.

Reading – *John 19.25–7*

Meanwhile, standing near the cross of Jesus were his mother, and his mother's sister, Mary the wife of Clopas, and Mary Magdalene. When Jesus saw his mother and the disciple whom he loved standing beside her, he said to his mother, 'Woman, here is your son.' Then he said to the disciple, 'Here is your mother.' And from that hour the disciple took her into his own home.

Reflection

This word from the cross shows us Jesus' very human heart and his care for his mother and the beloved disciple, John. These two have come with him all the way, even to the foot of the cross, their grief has brought them together and Jesus asks them to care for one another when he is dead. 'Woman, here is your son; Son, here is your mother.' In the face of his own death Jesus is creating new bonds of family and relationship, new levels of interdependence.

From a place of pain, it is Jesus who is seeking to protect and care for his loved ones, to help them to know that they each have a purpose and a responsibility to each other after his death. It echoes his life's work, of bringing isolated and unloved people together into new communities of care. 'Look after my mum' is a very human response to an appalling situation.

These new relationships are based not upon ties of blood and family, but are creating a new family of choice. A community project can see volunteers coming together, some very lonely, some with disabilities, yet each with so much to give. A common endeavour and strong sense of belonging can be like a family, creating a basic building block for repairing communities. When so much is fractured and broken, Jesus longs for us to belong together in intentional communities of love.

Music – *suggestions*

Gabriel Fauré, Requiem, Pie Jesu

The poet acts, Philip Glass

The Seven Last Words, Sonata III (extract 4 minutes), Haydn

Silence *(about four minutes)*

We take into the silence:
memories of our own loss, grief, aloneness
the picture of our own circle of friends and family
the challenge of where are we being called into new community.

After the silence we respond
Be strong, and let your heart take courage,
all you who wait for the Lord.
Psalm 31.24

Prayer

Lord Jesus,
You draw us into new patterns
of relationship and care.
You help us to rebuild our broken communities
through your generous, inclusive love.
Help us now to open our hearts and our homes
to find new ways to belong together
within the promise of your kingdom.
Amen.

Hymn/Song/Chant – *suggestions*

Do not be afraid, for I have redeemed you, Gerard Markland

Goodness is stronger than evil, Desmond Tutu and John L. Bell (WGRG)

Within our darkest night, Taizé Community

Morning glory, H. Vanstone

I am thirsty

Our real needs
Being able to receive from others

Introduction

So we come to the second word from the cross, Jesus cries out in pain and need.

Reading – *John 19.28–9*

After this, when Jesus knew that all was now finished, he said (in order to fulfill the scripture), 'I am thirsty.' A jar full of sour wine was standing there. So they put a sponge full of the wine on a branch of hyssop and held it to his mouth.

Reflection

This word from the cross speaks of real human need, the most basic need of all. In the heat of the sun and wracked by pain, Jesus cries out 'I thirst', I am thirsty, give me a drink. He who is the living water, bubbling up for others to find life, he is thirsty – and these words express that need.

Jesus lived a life of generous giving, he poured himself out for others. But he was not afraid to name and know his own real needs. He was not afraid to ask for help. In this cry from the cross, 'I am thirsty', we see his willingness to receive, and to be needy.

In a world of competence, which prizes strength and ability and self-reliance, these words can encourage us to acknowledge our own incompetence and vulnerability, our own real needs. It's sometimes hard for us to recognize what we really need. There are so many things that we think we want in life, consumer products to pamper and comfort us, luxuries to build up our self-esteem, so many inessentials that crowd in on us. All these diversions camouflage our real needs and leave us diminished or dissatisfied.

It takes a certain level of humility to receive from others; and we don't find it easy. It's important to learn how to give and receive with good grace.

Music – *suggestions*

Six Etudes for Piano: Etude 5, Philip Glass

Seven last words: I thirst (extract 4 minutes), James MacMillan

The Seven Last Words, Sonata V (extract 4 minutes), Haydn

Silence *(about four minutes)*

We take into the silence –
our own dryness and thirst
our own deepest needs
an openness to receive

After the silence we respond
Be strong, and let your heart take courage,
all you who wait for the Lord.
Psalm 31.24

Prayer

Gracious God
You know our deepest needs,
help us to hear them too.
Amid the clamouring voices of
want and desire,
we thirst for your
unconditional love,
help us to receive you now.
Amen.

Hymn/Song/Chant – *suggestions*

As the deer longs for the water, Martyn Nystrom

In Christ alone, Keith Getty and Stuart Townend

I heard the voice of Jesus say, Horatius Bonar

Jesus, remember me, Taizé Community

It is finished

Honest endings
Recognizing death and what has been accomplished

Introduction

In our final word from the cross, Jesus knows that the end is near
and calls out.

Reading – *John 19.30*

When Jesus had received the wine, he said, 'It is finished.'
Then he bowed his head and gave up his spirit.

Reflection

The last word from the cross in St John's Gospel: 'It is finished.' The horror is over, it is accomplished, the work is done. In the eyes of the world, this is the moment of absolute failure; but in the purposes of God, this is the consummation of an act of unconditional love for the world. These words don't imply a defeated sense of relief that Jesus' suffering is over, his life is ending: the Greek word *tetelestai* is a word with a strong, triumphant ring, 'It is accomplished.' 'It is complete.'

In hospital, where the doctors fight for every moment of life for a patient, death can easily be seen as a failure. Hospices have reminded us of the possibility of a 'good death', of being able to let go into the ultimate healing of heaven. We sometimes speak of winning or losing the battle against illness. The real accomplishment may be the willing acceptance of the disintegration, letting go into death, to find deeper integration in the depths of God's love.

For Jesus, there is recognition in the words 'It is finished' that death comes as the completion of a life lived to the full, offered for others. And as we understand this more fully, perhaps it even helps us to face our own death without fear. We may even ultimately be able to see death as a friend, leading us home, as St Francis does in his 'Canticle of the Sun': 'And thou most kind and gentle death, waiting to hush our latest breath, thou leadest home the child of God, and Christ himself that way has trod.'

Music – *suggestions*

The Seven Last Words, Sonata VI (extract of 4 minutes), Haydn

The Seven Last Words, It is finished (extract of 4 minutes), James MacMillan

Silence *(about four minutes)*

We take into the silence:
our own sense of mortality,

our own accomplishments,
an openness to what lies beyond our horizon.

After the silence we respond
Be strong, and let your heart take courage,
all you who wait for the Lord.
Psalm 31.24

Prayer

Gracious God,
accomplish in us your purposes,
complete in us your work of healing love,
that, though we walk through the valley
of the shadow of death,
we may find you
one step ahead of us,
leading us home.
Amen.

Hymn/Song/Chant – *suggestions*

In our darkness, Taizé Community

Drop, drop, slow tears, Phineas Fletcher

Night has fallen, John L. Bell (WGRG)

Faithful one, Brian Doerksen

Reading – *John 19.31–42*

Since it was the day of Preparation, the Jews did not want the bodies left on the cross during the sabbath, especially because that sabbath was a day of great solemnity. So they asked Pilate to have the legs of the crucified men broken and the bodies removed. Then the soldiers came and broke the legs of the first and of the other who had been crucified with him. But when they came to Jesus and saw that he was already dead, they did not break his legs. Instead, one of the soldiers pierced his side with a spear, and at once blood and water came out. (He who saw this has testified so that you also may believe. His testimony is true, and he knows that he tells the truth.) These things occurred so that the scripture might be fulfilled, 'None of his bones shall be broken.' And again another passage of scripture says, 'They will look on the one whom they have pierced.'

After these things, Joseph of Arimathea, who was a disciple of Jesus, though a secret one because of his fear of the Jews, asked Pilate to let him take away the body of Jesus. Pilate gave him permission; so he came and removed his body. Nicodemus, who had at first come to Jesus by night, also came, bringing a mixture of myrrh and aloes, weighing about a hundred pounds. They took the body of Jesus and wrapped it with the spices in linen cloths, according to the burial custom of the Jews. Now there was a garden in the place where he was crucified, and in the garden there was a new tomb in which no one had ever been laid. And so, because it was the Jewish day of Preparation, and the tomb was nearby, they laid Jesus there.

Prayer

Gracious God,
your hands now bear the wounds,
your heart now holds the agony,
of that appalling cross.
Hold us in your everlasting arms
as we face the little deaths of daily life
and the great mystery of our own mortality.
May we find you there beside us,
light in our darkest night.
Amen.

Hymn

The Wonder of the Cross, Vicky Beeching

When I survey the wondrous cross, Isaac Watts

I cannot tell, William Young Fullerton

The Cross of Christ

You took our worst:
you gave your best.
You took our hate:
you gave your love.
You took that cross:
you changed everything.
We adore you, O Christ,
and we bless you.

As music is played we come up to the cross to give thanks and
to pray
Some may simply stand, others may hold or kiss the cross
In whatever way we feel comfortable, we honour the cross

Music – *suggestion*

The Armed Man: Benedictus, Karl Jenkins

We leave the church in silence.

EASTER SEASON

Holy Saturday

Called to wait
Loss and grief, harrowing our hearts

Introduction

This is a short reflective service of patient waiting in the darkness of the night. You might like to invite people who have been bereaved, or been through a profound loss or illness, through unemployment or separation. In the same way that some have offered a 'Blue Christmas' service, Holy Saturday can offer an Easter alternative for those who cannot yet get to the resurrection joy of Easter Day. At the heart of this service we will build a cairn of stones, echoing the stone rolled in front of Jesus' tomb. You will need to provide some suitable stones that people could choose as they come in;

*larger ones would be best. You will need to create a place for a
cairn to be built, perhaps a raised platform to help those with
limited mobility. Beside it, set up a place to light votive candles,
enough for everybody to light one, with tapers ready for lighting.*

Gathering Music – *suggestion*

De Profundis, Arvo Pärt

Welcome

Tonight we stand with Mary Magdalene, with Joseph of
Arimathea, and with all the disciples who have watched Jesus die.
Like them, we come in shock and sorrow, in aching loss and grief,
knowing that we are powerless in the face of death. All we can do
is watch and wait, praying for the dawning of a new day. Unlike
Mary Magdalene, Joseph of Arimathea and the disciples, we know
the story of Easter Day, we know the promise of resurrection; but
sometimes in grief it is hard to reach that place. It is a long journey, and we can only plod on through the 'valley of the shadow
of death', holding the hope that this is not the end of the story.

Hymn/Song/Chant – *suggestions*

Were you there when they crucified my Lord? Traditional
Spiritual

Stay here with me, remain here with me, Taizé Community

Empty, broken, here I stand, The Northumbria Community

Be still my soul, Kathrina von Schlegel, trans. Jane Borthwick

Opening Prayer

In the darkness of the night,
in the depths of our sorrow,
when the worst has happened,
Stay with us, Lord Jesus.

When love has been killed,
when hope has been trampled,
when joy has been extinguished,
Stay with us, Lord Jesus.

When nothing can be done,
when we are powerless to change events,
when all has been lost,
Stay with us, Lord Jesus.

Stay with us,
as we wait with you,
hold us steady in this place of pain:
Stay with us, Lord Jesus.

Jesus says, 'I will never leave you or forsake you.'
So we can say with confidence,
'The Lord is my helper; I will not be afraid.
What can anyone do to me?'
Hebrews 13.5b–6

Reading – *Psalm 130*

Out of the depths I cry to you, O Lord.
Lord, hear my voice!
Let your ears be attentive
to the voice of my supplications!
If you, O Lord, should mark iniquities,
Lord, who could stand?
But there is forgiveness with you,
so that you may be revered.
I wait for the Lord, my soul waits,
and in his word I hope;
my soul waits for the Lord
more than those who watch for the morning,
more than those who watch for the morning.

O Israel, hope in the Lord!
For with the Lord there is steadfast love,
and with him is great power to redeem.
It is he who will redeem Israel
from all its iniquities.
Glory to the Father and to the Son and to the Holy Spirit;
As it was in the beginning, is now, and shall be for ever. Amen.

Reading – *Matthew 27.57–61*

When it was evening, there came a rich man from Arimathea, named Joseph, who was also a disciple of Jesus. He went to Pilate and asked for the body of Jesus; then Pilate ordered it to be given to him. So Joseph took the body and wrapped it in a clean linen cloth and laid it in his own new tomb, which he had hewn in the rock. He then rolled a great stone to the door of the tomb and went away. Mary Magdalene and the other Mary were there, sitting opposite the tomb.

Living word of God,
Live in our lives today.

Reflection

Mary Magdalene and the other Mary sit opposite the huge stone. They are powerless, they can do nothing to change what has happened. All they can do is wait. For all who have walked through the valley of the shadow of death, for all who have watched a loved one die, this is a familiar place. It is the kind of waiting we know between a death and a funeral. We may feel numb, cold, empty. It may feel like a nightmare, we can hardly believe it has happened. In all our losses – redundancy, illness, separation – we come closer to the depths of sadness and pain, sometimes of despair and loss. Out of the depths we cry for help. As we hold the stone we have chosen, we remember the stone-cold tomb; we stay with Mary in her vigil, allowing the stone to represent those depths to us.

Silence *(about five minutes)*

In the silence, as we hold our stone, we think of the times of sadness and pain, despair and loss that we have known.

Prayers of Recognition

When hopes have been crushed by fear,
when love has been overcome by hatred,
and death seems to have won the day,
(Silence)

out of the depths I cry to you, O Lord.
Lord, hear my voice!

When faith seems hollow and empty,
when we feel betrayed and let down,
and nothing makes sense any more,
(Silence)

out of the depths I cry to you, O Lord.
Lord, hear my voice!

When people seem distant and uncaring,
when we feel alone and abandoned,
and nobody seems to understand,
(Silence)

out of the depths I cry to you, O Lord.
Lord, hear my voice!

Lord, you have heard the cry of your people,
even in the darkest place you are with us,
even in the depths you still hold us.
(Silence)

I wait for the Lord, my soul waits,
and in his word I hope.

Despite everything, despite all that is broken,
despite all that seems cold and hard,
even in this place you still hold us.
(Silence)

I wait for the Lord, my soul waits,
and in his word I hope.

Lord, you have promised that this will not be the end.
We wait, hoping for the promised dawn of Easter morning,
when love and life will once again break through,
like the first flowers of spring after a long, hard winter.
(Silence)

I wait for the Lord, my soul waits,
and in his word I hope.

Hymn/Song/Chant – *suggestions*

Be still for the presence of the Lord, David J. Evans

Wait for the Lord, Taizé Community

From the falter of breath, John L. Bell (WGRG)

Reading – *Revelation 1.17–18*

When I saw him, I fell at his feet as though dead. But he placed
his right hand on me, saying, 'Do not be afraid; I am the first
and the last, and the living one. I was dead, and see, I am alive
forever and ever; and I have the keys of Death and of Hades.'

Living word of God,
Live in our lives today.

Reflection

One ancient tradition of the Church is that during this time between his death and resurrection, Jesus descended into the place of the dead to bring life to all who had died in past generations. This strong image has been called the 'harrowing of hell'; and it reminds us that there are no depths and no places beyond God's reach: God can bring life even to the toughest, most unlikely situations. To 'harrow' is to rake or hoe the soil, to break up the hardened pan, to create a friable loam in which seeds can germinate and grow. When we are overwhelmed with sadness or loss, when we experience darkness or depression, this is a promise to us too. God can 'harrow' even our deepest, darkest times. God can break up our hardened selves, to make it possible for new seeds to grow in us.

We are invited to bring our stone to form a cairn. In putting our stone in the cairn, we lay down the burdens we have been carrying; and we open ourselves to God, allowing him to 'harrow' us, trusting that new shoots of life will emerge. We then light a candle of hope for resurrection life.

Music – *suggestion*

De Profundis, Arvo Pärt

As the music plays we bring our stones to form a cairn, a marker on our journey, a place of solidarity with all who carry heavy burdens of loss
As we each place our stone we pray:
Spirit of God, harrow our hearts, bless us with new life.

We light a candle of hope for resurrection life, embracing earth and heaven, reaching beyond death to life

Closing Responses

As we wait for the morning, for the hope of a new dawn,
Roll away the stone!
As we face the tomb of our loss and grief, wondering how to
move on,
Roll away the stone!
As we remember the promise of resurrection life, unsure of how
it will come,
Roll away the stone!

Blessing

Christ whom death could not contain,
roll away the heavy stone of our grief and sadness.
Harrow all that has become hardened in us and
open our hearts to the possibilities of new life.
Father, Son, Spirit,
Bless us in unexpected ways,
with your gift of resurrection life.
Amen.

Hymn/Song/Chant – *suggestions*

Behold, behold, I make all things new, John L. Bell (WGRG)

Now the green blade riseth, John Macleod Campbell Crum

See, what a morning, Keith Getty, Stuart Townend

Easter Day

Called to be alive
Not living and partly living, but fully alive

Introduction

You will need to set up a rough cross that will be decorated with flowers and greenery during the service. To make it easy to attach flowers to the cross, you may need either to wrap it in chicken wire or to create a criss-cross of wires. You may like to encourage people to bring yellow and white flowers and green foliage from their gardens, as well as providing some spare for visitors. The flowers and foliage can be set near to the cross on a table.

Gathering Music – *suggestions*

Easter Oratorio, Bach

Petrushka, Stravinsky

Welcome

To every human tyrant and dictator, to every war monger and oppressor, today is a fearful day. To every religious bigot and extremist, to every fundamentalist, today is a fearful day. We come to celebrate the liberation of the human spirit! We come to celebrate the triumph of love over hate, the triumph of life over death, the triumph of good over evil. For today the power of the cross is broken, the power of fear and despair is defeated. Because of today we can dare to hope, we can dare to believe. Jesus, who was killed on the cross, is risen. Jesus, who was lain in a tomb, is alive. Come, let us celebrate the feast!

Pascal Candle

A new candle is lit to celebrate the light of Christ.
The light shines in the darkness,
and the darkness did not overcome it.
Alleluia, Christ is risen!
He is risen indeed, alleluia!
John 1.5

Hymn/Song/Chant – *suggestions*

Jesus Christ is risen today, Lyra Davidica

O happy day, Tim Hughes

He is risen, he is risen! Noel Richards

Clap your hands all you nations, John L. Bell (WGRG)

Canticle Responses

So if you have been raised with Christ,
seek the things that are above,
where Christ is, seated at the right hand of God.
Set your minds on things that are above,
not on things that are on earth,
for you have died, and your life is hidden with Christ in God.
When Christ who is your life is revealed,
then you also will be revealed with him in glory.
Glory to the Father and to the Son and to the Holy Spirit;
as it was in the beginning, is now and shall be for ever. Amen.
Colossians 3.1–4

Opening Prayer

Risen Lord Jesus,
present with us now,
open our hearts to receive you,
open our minds to understand you,
ignite our will to follow you.
Bring your resurrection life to all that is dead in us,
your living hope to all that despairs,
your risen joy to all that is sorrowful,
bring your love to transform our living.
May our lives touch all those we meet,
that all your children may come to know you,
to be their life, joy, hope and love.
Amen.

Reading – *John 20.1–10*

Early on the first day of the week, while it was still dark, Mary
Magdalene came to the tomb and saw that the stone had been
removed from the tomb. So she ran and went to Simon Peter and
the other disciple, the one whom Jesus loved, and said to them,
'They have taken the Lord out of the tomb, and we do not know
where they have laid him.' Then Peter and the other disciple set

out and went toward the tomb. The two were running together, but the other disciple outran Peter and reached the tomb first. He bent down to look in and saw the linen wrappings lying there, but he did not go in. Then Simon Peter came, following him, and went into the tomb. He saw the linen wrappings lying there, and the cloth that had been on Jesus' head, not lying with the linen wrappings but rolled up in a place by itself. Then the other disciple, who reached the tomb first, also went in, and he saw and believed; for as yet they did not understand the scripture, that he must rise from the dead. Then the disciples returned to their homes.

Living Word of God,
Live in our lives today.

Reflection

Death is so disorienting, and we rarely know what to do. It was no different for the disciples.

There is so much rushing about in this account, running, misunderstanding, jumping to conclusions. There is a preoccupation with the place of death, the details of exactly where the linen wrappings are all placed. In the frenetic activity it is no wonder that 'they did not understand'! In the end, they just go home again.

In every kind of loss, in death, in separation, unemployment, disability and illness, it is easy for us to get stuck in the place of loss. But new life isn't usually to be found in the tomb. So inevitably there is a sense of dislocation, as we focus on the tomb and wonder where life will emerge. And the new life may well surprise us in unexpected places, and in unlooked for people and ways.

For a moment we pause to think of where we are looking for life but not finding it, where we are rushing about and getting nowhere!

Silence *(about two minutes)*

Conversation

We turn to our neighbour to share what this reading touched in us

Hymn/Song/Chant – *suggestions*

Behold, behold, I make all things new, John L. Bell (WGRG)

Jubilate everybody, Fred Dunn

Reading – *John 20.11–18*

But Mary stood weeping outside the tomb. As she wept, she bent over to look into the tomb; and she saw two angels in white, sitting where the body of Jesus had been lying, one at the head and the other at the feet. They said to her, 'Woman, why are you weeping?' She said to them, 'They have taken away my Lord, and I do not know where they have laid him.' When she had said this, she turned around and saw Jesus standing there, but she did not know that it was Jesus. Jesus said to her, 'Woman, why are you weeping? For whom are you looking?' Supposing him to be the gardener, she said to him, 'Sir, if you have carried him away, tell me where you have laid him, and I will take him away.' Jesus said to her, 'Mary!' She turned and said to him in Hebrew, 'Rabbouni!' (which means Teacher). Jesus said to her, 'Do not hold on to me, because I have not yet ascended to the Father. But go to my brothers and say to them, "I am ascending to my Father and your Father, to my God and your God."' Mary Magdalene went and announced to the disciples, 'I have seen the Lord'; and she told them that he had said these things to her.

Living Word of God,
Live in our lives today.

Hymn/Song/Chant – *suggestions*

Led like a lamb, Graham Kendrick

Love's redeeming work is done, Charles Wesley

Alleluia, Taizé Community

Reflection

After all the rushing about Mary stops and simply weeps. Tears are the most authentic and real thing that we can do in the face of death and loss. It doesn't matter how much faith we have, you can't short circuit grief. Sometimes it is only when we break down and cry that we can face the pain and acknowledge, there is nothing we can do in the face of this situation. It is through her tears that Mary begins to see her way through, to glimpse the possibility of new life. At first she is confused, thinking Jesus is the gardener, but when he says her name Mary recognizes Jesus. Easter Day is about this breaking through to a new beginning. After all sorts of loss, the breakup of a relationship, the loss of a job, or of our health, and of course after a bereavement, we can find ourselves disoriented and confused. But the good news of Easter is that Jesus' death was not the end of the story, that hatred is not the end of the story, that evil is not the end of the story: beyond those, there is confusion and disorientation, through which, somehow, transformative life and love and goodness can break through.

Finally recognizing Jesus, Mary is commissioned to be the first Apostle, sent by Jesus to take the good news of his resurrection to the other disciples.

Easter Day starts with confusion, brings us to tears, opens our eyes to a new possibility, and finally commissions us for a new life.

Silence *(two minutes)*

We reflect on the journey from confusion and tears to new possibilities and commissioning for new life.

Conversation

We turn to our neighbour to share what this reading touched in us

Hymn/Song/Chant – *suggestions*

Sent by the Lord am I, Jorge Maldonado

Send me out, Steve Fee

You have called us by our name, Bernadette Farrell

Prayers of Recognition

When we are rushing about, frenetic, over-busy,
jumping to conclusions and confusions,
God be our still point.
(Silence)

We have seen the Lord.
Amen. Alleluia!

When we are consumed with sorrow, and overcome with tears,
hurting and lost, unable to see our way forward,
God be our still point.
(Silence)

We have seen the Lord.
Amen. Alleluia!

When we cannot recognize you, when we have lost our way,
speak our name, help us to hear.
God be our still point.
(Silence)

We have seen the Lord.
Amen. Alleluia!

When we begin to glimpse the new possibilities of resurrection
life,
commission us, sending us out with confidence to speak and live
for you.
God be our still point.
(Silence)

We have seen the Lord.
Amen. Alleluia!

Prayers of Intercession

We think of the tomb,
and of all that speaks of death and destruction in our world.
We pray for nations in conflict,
for the hunger and disruption that comes with war.
We pray for the environmental catastrophe of global warming,
    and our part in it.
In the place of pain and loss
we dare to affirm the hope of the blessings of Easter.

We think of the disciples' confusion, and pointless rushing about.
We pray for all who are over-busy,
burnt out, exhausted trying to make ends meet.
We pray for the under-employed,
and those forced into inactivity by disability.
In the place of pain and loss
we dare to affirm the hope of the blessings of Easter.

We think of Mary not recognizing Jesus,
then hearing him call her name.
We pray for the lonely, unloved and abandoned,
especially those with mental illness.
We pray for the homeless, vulnerable and afraid,
for all who go unnoticed.
In the place of pain and loss
we dare to affirm the hope of the blessings of Easter.

We think of Jesus sending Mary to the disciples
with the good news of resurrection life.
We pray for all who long for that good news today,
the sick and suffering, all who grieve.
We remember those who have died ....
In the place of pain and loss
we dare to affirm the hope of the blessings of Easter.

We make our own deepest prayers now as we come to decorate the cross, allowing each flower or sprig to signify a person or situation we bring to the cross of Christ.

Decorating the Cross

As a piece of music is played, we are invited to bring flowers and sprigs of foliage to the cross and to decorate it
People may like to join in with the singing

Music – *suggestion*

O Lord, hear my prayer, Taizé Community

Once everyone is seated, again we say:
In the place of pain and loss
we dare to affirm the hope of the blessings of Easter.
In the place of horror and shame
we dare to share the beauty of Easter.
In the place of death and sorrow
we dare to celebrate the life and love of Easter.

Hymn/Song/Chant – *suggestions*

Thine be the glory, Edmond Budry

See, what a morning, Keith Getty, Stuart Townend

We walk his way (Ewe Thina), trans. Anders Nyberg and Sven-Bernhard Fast

Blessing

Therefore, if anyone is in Christ,
we are a new creation;
the old has gone,
the new has come!
1 Corinthians 5

God of new possibilities,
new beginning, new hope,
bless us now with your resurrection life!
Jesus, calling us by name,
knowing and loving us completely,
bless us now with your resurrection life!
Spirit, sending us out with Good News,
equipping and energizing us,
bless us now with your resurrection life!
The blessing of God,
Father, Son and Holy Spirit,
be with us and remain with us
now and for ever.
Amen.

Bread of Hospitality

Agapé on the Road to Emmaus

Introduction

This service can be set within the context of a full meal, and people can be invited to bring and share food together. It can be an opportunity to bring together people who might not usually meet one another. Equally the service can simply conclude with the sharing of bread. You will need to prepare a table for the Agapé. Also, you will need four symbols – a cross, a Bible, a candle and a loaf of bread – and four people to introduce each symbol with the words suggested in the service.

Gathering Music – *suggestion*

I can see (Emmaus Road), Gloria Gaither with David Meece

Alleluia, Christ is risen!
He is risen indeed, Alleluia!

Welcome

With the benefit of hindsight, the Easter story can be celebrated with joy; but to those who had been so recently traumatized by the arrest, torture and death of their leader and friend Jesus, it is hard to comprehend or believe all that was being reported.

Hymn/Song/Chant – *suggestions*

All are welcome, Marty Haughen

Brother, sister let me serve you, Richard Gillard

One more step, Sydney Carter

Opening Prayer

Hear my prayer, O Lord;
let my cry come to you.
Do not hide your face from me
in the day of my distress.
Incline your ear to me;
answer me speedily in the day when I call.
Psalm 102.1–2

God of encounter,
you meet us in our confusion and loss,
even when we run away from you.
Walk with us on the road,
hear our hurts and regrets,
help us to let go of the past,
and to recognize you in unexpected ways.
We ask this in the name of Jesus
who comes to us in the face of a stranger.
Amen.

Bible Reading – *Luke 24.13–35*

Now on that same day two of them were going to a village called Emmaus, about seven miles from Jerusalem, and talking with each other about all these things that had happened. While they were talking and discussing, Jesus himself came near and went with them, but their eyes were kept from recognizing him. And he said to them, 'What are you discussing with each other while you walk along?' They stood still, looking sad. Then one of them, whose name was Cleopas, answered him, 'Are you the only stranger in Jerusalem who does not know the things that have taken place there in these days?' He asked them, 'What things?' They replied, 'The things about Jesus of Nazareth, who was a prophet mighty in deed and word before God and all the people, and how our chief priests and leaders handed him over to be condemned to death and crucified him. But we had hoped that he was the one to redeem Israel. Yes, and besides all this, it is now the third day since these things took place. Moreover, some women of our group astounded us. They were at the tomb early this morning, and when they did not find his body there, they came back and told us that they had indeed seen a vision of angels who said that he was alive. Some of those who were with us went to the tomb and found it just as the women had said; but they did not see him.' Then he said to them, 'Oh, how foolish you are, and how slow of heart to believe all that the prophets have declared! Was it not necessary that the Messiah should suffer these things and then enter into his glory?' Then beginning with Moses and all the prophets, he interpreted to them the things about himself in all the scriptures.

Living Word of God,
Live in us today.

Reflection

After the terrible trauma of Jesus' arrest, trial and execution, the disciples are disorientated, confused, afraid of arrest themselves, desperately trying to make sense of all they have been through. A stranger meets them on the road and asks them why they are so sad. They pour out their story to him; and in doing so, they begin on the path to healing.

In our busy, defended world, how often do we notice the sadness of strangers, and dare to ask them why? Like the Priests and Levites in the parable of the Good Samaritan, we often keep our eyes down and pass by on the other side. But Jesus calls us to a culture of encounter, even in the face of pain: do we have the courage to make time to reach out with the gift of time and a listening ear?

Jesus shows the power of simple questions to unlock the depth of another person's story, the reality of their pain. 'What are you discussing?' 'What things?' These simple questions stop the disciples in their tracks. They unlock something, enabling the disciples to voice their sadness, and to begin to let go of the trauma.

'But we had hoped he was the one.' Voicing their disappointment and loss is the first step on the path of letting go into new life.

Silence *(about three minutes)*

Is there room in your life to stop and listen to a stranger?
Is there sadness you find it hard to let go of and need to name?

Prayers of Recognition

We bring to you our hopes that have been disappointed,
the sadness we find hard to name or to let go.
(Silence)

Hear my prayer, O Lord;
let my cry come to you.

We bring to you the long and lonely roads we have trodden,
the times we have walked away bemused.
(Silence)

Hear my prayer, O Lord;
let my cry come to you.

We bring to you the times we have been too busy to listen,
the people who we have missed.
(Silence)

Hear my prayer, O Lord;
let my cry come to you.

Hymn/Song/Chant – *suggestions*

O Lord, whose love designed this day, Christopher Idle

Haven't you heard that Jesus is risen, Alison Robertson

Wonder and stare, fear and beware, John L. Bell (WGRG)

O Lord, hear my prayer, Taizé Community

Bible Reading – *Luke 24.28–35*

As they came near the village to which they were going, he walked
ahead as if he were going on. But they urged him strongly, saying, 'Stay with us, because it is almost evening and the day is
now nearly over.' So he went in to stay with them. When he was
at the table with them, he took bread, blessed and broke it, and
gave it to them. Then their eyes were opened, and they recognized him; and he vanished from their sight. They said to each
other, 'Were not our hearts burning within us while he was talking to us on the road, while he was opening the scriptures to us?'
That same hour they got up and returned to Jerusalem; and they
found the eleven and their companions gathered together. They
were saying, 'The Lord has risen indeed, and he has appeared
to Simon!' Then they told what had happened on the road, and
how he had been made known to them in the breaking of the
bread.

Living Word of God,
Live in our lives today.

Reflection

The disciples had learned the practice of hospitality from Jesus. Breaking bread was a way of encountering each other, of including the outcast and unloved. As the stranger made to go on, they urged him to stay. They opened the possibility of a deeper encounter, and of recognizing Jesus in the taking, blessing, breaking and sharing of bread. Their eyes were opened! Breaking bread, sharing hospitality, opens our eyes to the presence of Christ among us. It changes the way we read the scriptures, it takes us on a journey from head to heart, from thinking *about* God to relationship *with* God.

Silence *(about three minutes)*

Where do we include strangers in our hospitality?
'Moving from head to heart': what does that mean for you?

Prayers of Intercession

We bring to you those who are not included,
the homeless, the disturbed, the different.
(Silence)

Stay with us;
Open our eyes to see you.

We bring to you those we do not recognize,
the stranger, the asylum seeker, the refugee.
(Silence)

Stay with us;
Open our minds to know you.

We bring to you those we find difficult,
the confused, the challenging, the disruptive.
(Silence)

Stay with us;
Open our hearts to love you.

Peace

'Were not our hearts burning within us while he was talking to
us on the road?'
The Peace of the Lord be always with you,
And also with you!
We exchange a sign of peace

Hymn/Song/Chant – *suggestions*

Guide me O thou great Redeemer, William Williams, trans.
Peter Williams

See, what a morning! Keith Getty, Stuart Townend

Glory and gratitude and praise, John L. Bell (WGRG)

Eat this bread, drink this cup, Taizé Community

Agapé Meal

The table is set with symbols of our faith

A Cross is set on the table as these words are spoken:
I bring a cross, to remind us of 'Jesus of Nazareth, who was a
prophet mighty in deed and word before God and all the people,
and how our chief priests and leaders handed him over to be
condemned to death and crucified him.'

An open Bible is set on the table as these words are spoken:
I bring a Bible to remind us that, 'beginning with Moses and all
the prophets, he interpreted to them the things about himself in
all the scriptures.'

A lit candle is set on the table as these words are spoken:
I bring a candle to remind us, 'Were not our hearts burning
within us while he was talking to us on the road?'

A loaf of bread is set on the table as these words are spoken:
I bring bread to remind us that 'When he was at the table with
them, he took bread, blessed and broke it, and gave it to them.'

Prayer of Thanksgiving

The leader takes the bread and says:
We give thanks to God for bread to break and companions to
share it.

The people respond:
Stay with us, Lord Jesus Christ.
Open our eyes to recognize you
in the breaking of bread,
in the faces of strangers,
in the sharing of hospitality.
May our hearts burn within us
with the power of your extravagant love.
Amen.

The bread is passed between the people, each breaking a piece
for their neighbour
If a full meal is to be shared, this continues at this point

Final Prayer

Bread of Life,
you come to us whenever we break bread in your name.
You bring us together,
friend and stranger,
young and old,
rich and poor,
wise and foolish,
devout and sceptic,
to open our eyes to you,
present in the heart of our community.

As we journey on,
may we be open to receive
the unexpected gift of your love from others
and may your love overflow in us
to be shared with others we encounter.
Propel us from this table
to go out with good news on our lips
and renewed hope in our hearts,
in Jesus' name we pray.
Amen.

Blessing

God of every encounter,
open our eyes to your presence among us,
in the meeting of strangers,
in the sharing of scriptures,
in the gift of hospitality,
in the breaking of bread.
Bless us
with eyes to recognize you,
with hearts to burn within us,
and with confidence to share your resurrection life.
Amen.

Hymn/Song/Chant – *suggestions*

I am the bread of life, Suzanne Toolan

Sent by the Lord am I, Jorge Maldonaldo

Behold, behold, I make all things new, John L. Bell (WGRG)

Behind Locked Doors

Overcoming fear and doubt

Introduction

For this service you will need a card strip suitable to use as a bookmark for each person attending, with some pens for writing. If these are given to people as they gather for worship, they can be used in the silences. One side of the card should read at the top, 'What is locked up in me?' and the other side should read, 'What is unlocked in me?'
You will also need to set up a place for anointing, with some oil for anointing.

Gathering Music – *suggestions*

The Trumpet Concerto, Henri Tomasi

Violin Concerto No. 1, Karol Szymanowski

These convey a mood of mystery and questioning that sets the scene for this service

Welcome

In the earliest days of Easter, the disciples were confused and frightened and met behind locked doors for fear of being arrested like Jesus. Today we are free to meet and to express our faith, but we can be constrained by other fears. Sometimes we are still fearful of talking about our faith in a secular society and in the world of work. Sometimes fear can sometimes lead us to hide our gifts and our deepest self, for lack of confidence. Sometimes questions of faith remain unexamined and hidden behind a locked door of 'certainty'. In this service we invite Jesus behind the locked doors, as we dare to open our whole selves to God.

Christ is risen,
He is risen indeed. Alleluia!

Hymn/Song/Chant – *suggestions*

In Christ alone, Keith Getty and Stuart Townend

Faithful one, so unchanging, Robin Mark

When our confidence is shaken, Fred Pratt Green

Nothing in height or in depth, John L. Bell (WGRG)

Opening Prayer

Risen Lord Jesus,
break through to the heart of us,
beneath the layers of protection,
the habitual armour of our public selves.
Unlock the hidden gifts,
the possibilities and hopes,
the unasked questions of faith and life in us.
Help us to breathe deeply of your Holy Spirit,
to be set free to grow into our truest selves
and to share that freedom with all those we meet.
Amen.

Canticle

Listen! I am standing at the door, knocking;
if you hear my voice and open the door,
I will come in to you and eat with you,
and you with me.
To the one who conquers
I will give a place with me on my throne,

just as I myself conquered
and sat down with my Father on his throne.
Let anyone who has an ear listen
to what the Spirit is saying to the churches.
Revelation 3.20–2

Glory to the Father and to the Son and to the Holy Spirit.
As it was in the beginning, is now and shall be for ever. Amen.

Reading – *John 20.19–23*

> When it was evening on that day, the first day of the week, and
> the doors of the house where the disciples had met were locked
> for fear of the Jews, Jesus came and stood among them and
> said, 'Peace be with you.' After he said this, he showed them his
> hands and his side. Then the disciples rejoiced when they saw
> the Lord. Jesus said to them again, 'Peace be with you. As the
> Father has sent me, so I send you.' When he had said this, he
> breathed on them and said to them, 'Receive the Holy Spirit. If
> you forgive the sins of any, they are forgiven them; if you retain
> the sins of any, they are retained.'

Living Word of God,
Live in our lives today.

Reflection

Fear turns us in on ourselves! There are churches where the doors
are locked once the congregation are gathered, and not just in
some far off dictatorship, but here in modern Britain! We may
find we operate behind closed doors when it comes to our faith,
finding it hard to speak openly of faith at work or among friends
and family. On a personal level, fear can mean that we never dare
to develop our gifts or explore a new possibility. Often, we are
afraid of failure, or ridicule, or just of change! But locked doors
are no obstacle to Jesus. As he came and stood among the fearful
disciples, so he comes to open the doors of hope in us!

Silence *(about three minutes)*

What is locked up in you? What gifts or opportunities have you closed down? Why?
Is your faith locked up behind closed doors? What might help to open any closed doors?

Prayers of Recognition

We bring to you all that is locked up in us,
all that is fearful in us,
all that prevents us from being fully ourselves.
(Silence)

Peace be with you.
Open the doors of hope in us.

We bring to you the gifts that we have yet to explore,
the new opportunities that daunt us,
all that we could be.
(Silence)

Peace be with you.
Open the doors of hope in us.

We bring to you our faith,
the times we find difficult to speak of it,
to find the right words or actions.
(Silence)

Peace be with you.
Open the doors of hope in us.

Hymn/Song/Chant – *suggestions*

Open the eyes of my heart, Lord, Michael W Smith

Hear us from heaven, Jared Anderson

We shall go out with hope of resurrection, June Boyce-Tillman

Laudate omnes gentes, Taizé Community

Reading – *John* 20.24–9

But Thomas (who was called the Twin), one of the twelve, was not with them when Jesus came. So the other disciples told him, 'We have seen the Lord.' But he said to them, 'Unless I see the mark of the nails in his hands, and put my finger in the mark of the nails and my hand in his side, I will not believe.'

A week later his disciples were again in the house, and Thomas was with them. Although the doors were shut, Jesus came and stood among them and said, 'Peace be with you.' Then he said to Thomas, 'Put your finger here and see my hands. Reach out your hand and put it in my side. Do not doubt but believe.' Thomas answered him, 'My Lord and my God!' Jesus said to him, 'Have you believed because you have seen me? Blessed are those who have not seen and yet have come to believe.'

Reflection

The great gift of Thomas was his willingness to question and doubt! He was unwilling to go along with the crowd, or settle for a second-hand experience, simply to fit in. For him, faith had to be tested, it had to be robust. Questioning Thomas was the devout sceptic, a pioneer of the scientific method. 'Unless I see the mark of the nails in his hands, and put my finger in the mark of the nails and my hand in his side, I will not believe.' But his questioning paid off, he came to make the strongest affirmation of who Jesus was: 'My Lord and my God!' Sometimes our faith gets locked behind a door of 'certainty' where we are unwilling to subject it to the questions that science, history and experience can raise. We end up with a fragile faith that cannot be much help in a rough and tumble world.

Silence *(about three minutes)*

What are the questions about God that you avoid? Does your faith feel robust or fragile? Where could you dare to explore those questions?

Prayers of Intercession

God of science and discovery,
we pray for all who explore the limits of human knowledge,
for scientists, engineers, sceptics, and philosophers.
As we search for truth, may we open the door to you, who are
    all truth.
(Silence)

See my hands.
My Lord and my God.

God of certainty and doubt,
we pray for all who explore the limits of faith,
for people of faith, for searchers, for doubters.
As we search for meaning, may we open the door to you who
    gives all meaning.
(Silence)

See my hands.
My Lord and my God.

God of love and relationship,
we pray for all who explore the many patterns of human relating,
for families of all shapes, for friendships, for those who are alone.
As we search for connection and belonging, may we open the
    door to your love.
(Silence)

See my hands.
My Lord and my God.

Hymn/Song/Chant – *suggestions*

God, who stretched the spangled heavens, Catherine Cameron

God is love, his the care, Percy Dearmer

Praise the source of faith and learning, Thomas Troeger

In chaos and nothingness, David Lee

Easter Resolutions

For the next five minutes each person is encouraged to use the card 'bookmark' to identify 'What is locked up in me?' including any questions we are aware of that have yet to be faced. Then, making some Easter resolutions, use the other side to identify 'What is unlocked in me?' including any new gifts or new opportunities to explore.

Music is played – suggestion: picking up the gathering music used at the outset

Anointing

We bring our 'bookmarks', as we are anointed to unlock the doors and to go out with confidence and energy into the rough and tumble world of family, friendship, community and work.

A member of the congregation anoints the leader using the words:
'Peace be with you. Receive the Holy Spirit.'

The leader then anoints the congregation using the same words:
'Peace be with you. Receive the Holy Spirit.'

Hymn/Song/Chant – *suggestions*

Go forth and tell! James Edward Seddon

Send me out, Steve Fee

In love you summon, John L. Bell (WGRG)

How can I keep from singing? Robert Lowrey and Doris Plenn

Blessing

Risen Lord Jesus,
no tomb could hold you,
no door could shut you out.
Bless us with your presence,
fill us with your Spirit,
send us out
into your rough and tumble world,
to live and love with you!
Amen.

Ascension

Stretching our vision

Introduction

You will need to prepare enough triangular-shaped bunting flags for each person attending, possibly using different coloured craft paper. The paper should be thick enough to write on, with pens or coloured pencils to allow people to be creative. You will need a length of twine or string to attach the flags to, using staples or strong tape. To make the flags ascend you could either use a helium filled balloon or a loop of nylon fishing line already secured over a high point, ready to attach the bunting and to pull up.

Gathering Music – *suggestions*

Ascension Oratorio, Bach

The Lark Ascending, Ralph Vaughan Williams

Welcome

We come to celebrate the Ascension of Jesus, who calls us to be eyewitnesses of his resurrection life and who sends us out to the ends of the earth. He invites us to move from our own narrow understanding of faith and to embrace the breadth and depth of God's vision for the whole of creation.

Hymn/Song/Chant – *suggestions*

Hail the day that sees him rise, Charles Wesley

Will you come and follow me, John L. Bell (WGRG) and Graham Maule

King of Kings, Jarrod Cooper

Responses

God has gone up with a shout,
the Lord with the sound of a trumpet.
Sing praises to God, sing praises;
sing praises to our King, sing praises.
For God is the king of all the earth;
sing praises with a psalm.
Psalm 47.5–7

Opening Prayer

God of height and depth,
God of length and breadth,
give us power to comprehend your fullness,
give us love that surpasses knowledge,
open our minds, our hearts, our whole selves,
to worship you in spirit and in truth.
In Jesus' name we pray.
Amen.
After Ephesians 3

Reading – *Acts 1.6–11*

So when they had come together, they asked him, 'Lord, is this the time when you will restore the kingdom to Israel?' He replied, 'It is not for you to know the times or periods that the Father has set by his own authority. But you will receive power when the Holy Spirit has come upon you; and you will be my witnesses in Jerusalem, in all Judea and Samaria, and to the ends of the earth.' When he had said this, as they were watching, he was lifted up, and a cloud took him out of their sight. While he was going and they were gazing up toward heaven, suddenly two men in white robes stood by them. They said, 'Men of Galilee, why do you stand looking up toward heaven? This Jesus, who has been taken up from you into heaven, will come in the same way as you saw him go into heaven.'

Living Word of God,
Live in our lives today.

Reflection

Ascension Day is all about moving from narrowness to wideness, from constraint to freedom, from the particular to the universal. The disciples were still focused in on their narrow understanding of what Jesus was about, thinking in terms of restoring Israel. They could not yet imagine the scope of God's purpose that embraced the whole human race. 'You will be my witnesses in Jerusalem, in all Judea and Samaria, and to the ends of the earth.' They have to let go of Jesus to receive the outpouring of the Holy Spirit, empowering them for this new, expansive vision. We can so easily become narrowed in our own thinking and in our vision. We find it hard to imagine God's loving purpose for the whole of creation. We can become preoccupied with congregations and services, as if that is all that matters! Sometimes we have to let go of our familiar ways of relating to God to be able to grow into a new and expanded vision of God.

Silence *(about three minutes)*

What am I preoccupied with? Where does my vision need stretching?
What is God's vision for the human race, for all of creation?

Prayers of Recognition

We bring to God our own narrowness of focus,
our preoccupation with our own concerns.
(Silence)

You will be my witnesses,
To the end of the earth.

We bring to God the narrowness of our churches' vision,
our preoccupation with numbers, finance and buildings.
(Silence)

You will be my witnesses,
To the end of the earth.

We offer to God our imagination and our creativity,
that we may dare to dream dreams!
(Silence)

You will be my witnesses,
To the end of the earth.

We offer to God ourselves, that our horizons may be expanded,
That we may be eyewitnesses!
(Silence)

You will be my witnesses,
To the end of the earth.

Hymn/Song/Chant – *suggestions*

There's a wideness in God's mercy, Frederick William Faber

Sing of the Lord's goodness, Ernest Sands

Sent by the Lord am I, Jorge Maldonado

Wonder and stare, John L. Bell (WGRG)

Ascension Vision Bunting

We take our vision flags and write our hopes and dreams for ourselves, our church, our community, our nation, our world! We add them to the twine and, once all are attached, we watch them ascend!

Prayers of Intercession

God of all creation,
stretch our imagination to share your vision
of a world in balance and harmony.
Help us to care for our environment,
to repair the damage we have done
and to live sustainably in the future.
(Silence)

Holy Spirit come upon us.
Hear our prayer.

God of all nations,
expand our horizon to include your whole human family,
in your web of belonging.
Help us to build bridges of trust,
to resolve the conflicts that divide us
and to live peaceably with all.
(Silence)

Holy Spirit come upon us.
Hear our prayer.

God of the Church,
enlarge our understanding of your call to serve our community,
to think and act beyond our walls.
Help us to listen before we speak,
to include those who have felt excluded,
and to walk in the footsteps of Jesus.
(Silence)

Holy Spirit come upon us.
Hear our prayer.

God of our working,
broaden our faith to include every part of our lives,
not just the Sunday-best bits.
Help us to see you in both sacred and secular,
to discern your purpose in all we do
and to seek your justice.
(Silence)

Holy Spirit come upon us.
Hear our prayer.

God of our struggle,
deepen our compassion for all those who suffer,
all who are unhappy, lost or lonely.
Help us to reach out to all in need,
and to stand with them.
(Silence)

Holy Spirit come upon us.
Hear our prayer.

God of time and eternity,
of endings and new beginnings,
of death and life,
help all who grieve the loss of loved ones
to be held in your healing love.
(Silence)

Holy Spirit come upon us.
Hear our prayer.

Peace

Confounder of expectations, you break open our limitations!
Disturber of the peace, you bring a deeper peace!
The Peace of the risen and ascended Lord be always with you.
And also with you.

Responses

Now to him who by the power at work within us
is able to accomplish abundantly
far more than all we can ask or imagine,
to him be glory in the church
and in Christ Jesus to all generations,
forever and ever. Amen.
Ephesians 3.20–1

Blessing

God of absence and presence,
send your Holy Spirit,
restore our faith,
renew our vision,
redirect our action,
that we may follow you into new adventures,
and know your blessing,
Father, Son and Holy Spirit.
Amen.

Hymn/Song/Chant – *suggestions*

Be the God of all my Sundays, Martin E. Leckebusch

Be thou my vision, Eleanor Henrietta Hull and Mary Byrne

Resources

The Armed Man: Benedictus, Karl Jenkins

The Armed Man: Torches, Karl Jenkins
www.boosey.com/shop/ucat/100664?gclid=EAIaIQobChMIyer
HoqOF2wIVrrftCh1nfAf-EAAYASAAEgLRAvD_BwE

Ascension Oratorio, Bach
www.yourclassical.org/story/2017/04/13/daily-download-js-
bach--easter-oratorio-sinfonia

De Profundis, Antonio Salieri
www.prestoclassical.co.uk/w/122759/Antonio-Salieri-De-
profundis-clamavit

De Profundis, Arvo Pärt
www.amazon.co.uk/P%C3%A4rt-Profundis-Arvo/dp/
B0000007FL

The deer's cry, Arvo Pärt
www.amazon.co.uk/s/ref=nb_sb_noss?url=search-alias%3D
digital-music&field-keywords=arvo+part+The+deers+cry

Easter Oratorio, Bach
www.yourclassical.org/story/2017/04/13/daily-download-js-
bach--easter-oratorio-sinfonia

The Goldberg Variations, Glenn Gould, Bach
www.amazon.co.uk/Bach-Goldberg-Variations-Gould-
Remastered/dp/B014RHU56A/ref=sr_1_3?s=dmusic&ie=
UTF8&qid=1514478352&sr=1-3-mp3-albums-bar-strip-
o&keywords=goldberg+variations+glenn+gould

I can see (Emmaus Road), Gloria Gaither with David Meece
www.allmusic.com/song/i-can-see-on-the-emmaus-road-mto
000496384

The kiss, Joe Niemand
www.shazam.com/track/58056184/the-kiss

Kyrie Eleison, Chris Tomlin
www.google.co.uk/search?q=kyrie+eleison+chris+tom-
lin+mp3+download&rlz=1C1BEMX_enGB726GB728&oq=
Kyrie+Eleison+Chris+Tomlin&aqs=chrome.3.0l6.2839j0j8
&sourceid=chrome&ie=UTF-8

Lakme: Flower duet, Leo Delibes
www.yourclassical.org/story/2016/01/21/daily-download-leo-
delibes--lakme-flower-duet

Lament for Jerusalem, John Tavener
www.musicsalesclassical.com/composer/work/1567/14169

The Lark Ascending, Ralph Vaughan Williams
https://archive.org/details/VwTheLarkAscendingbeanBoult

Love each other, Graham Kendrick
www.grahamkendrick.co.uk/songs/graham-kendrick-songs/
banquet/love-each-other-all-the-room-was-hushed-and-still

Night, Einaudi
www.amazon.co.uk/Night/dp/B013FOV8FI

Nocturne in E Minor Op 72 No 1, Chopin
www.lisztonian.com/titles/Nocturne+in+E+Minor+Op+
72+No+1+posthumous-74.html

Our Lord, you were sent
www.carolynshymns.com/our_lord_you_were_sent.html

Pavan, William Byrd
www.last.fm/music/William+Byrd/_/Pavan

Petrushka, Igor Stravinsky
www.google.co.uk/search?q=petrushka+igor+stravinsky+
mp3+download&rlz=1C1BEMX_enGB726GB728&oq=
Petrushka+Igor+Stravinsky&aqs=chrome.3.ol6.3754joj8&
sourceid=chrome&ie=UTF-8

The poet acts, Philip Glass
www.amazon.com/The-Poet-Acts/dp/BoooUWFPDA

Prayer of the Heart, John Tavener
www.prestoclassical.co.uk/classical/products/7948222--john-
tavener-a-portrait

Requiem: Pie Jesu, Gabriel Fauré
www.yourclassical.org/story/2016/02/15/daily-download-
gabriel-faure--requiem-pie-jesu

St John Passion, Arvo Pärt
www.prestoclassical.co.uk/w/52822/Arvo-P%C3%A4rt-Passio-
St-John-Passion

Seraph II Adagio, James MacMillan
www.boosey.com/cr/music/James-MacMillan-Seraph/55964&
langid=1

The Seven Last Words, Sonata III, Haydn
myopenmp3.com/mp3/mo/music/285188686/joseph-haydn-the-
seven-last-words-of-our-saviour-on-the-cross-julius-rudel-the-
orchestra-of-st-luke-s-orchestra-of-st-luke-s-julius-rudel-mp3-
download

The Seven Last Words, Sonata V, Haydn
https://myopenmp3.com/mp3/mo/music/285188686/joseph-
haydn-the-seven-last-words-of-our-saviour-on-the-cross-julius-
rudel-the-orchestra-of-st-luke-s-orchestra-of-st-luke-s-julius-
rudel-mp3-download

The Seven Last Words, Sonata VI, Haydn
www.hyperion-records.co.uk/dc.asp?dc=D_CKD153

The Seven Last Words, I thirst, James MacMillan
www.hyperion-records.co.uk/dc.asp?dc=D_CDA67460

The Seven Last Words, It is finished, James MacMillan
www.hyperion-records.co.uk/dc.asp?dc=D_CDA67460

Six Etudes for Piano: Etude 5, Philip Glass
www.prestoclassical.co.uk/classical/works/274461--glass-p-piano-etude-no-5/browse

Stations of the Cross Visuals
https://www.paulineuk.org/browse/item/the-footsteps-of-Christ-poster-set/5031446738009
https://www.mccrimmons.com/way-of-the-cross

The Trumpet Concerto, Henri Tomasi
https://kupdf.com/download/henri-tomasi-trumpet-concerto_58e3ee22dcod60a20cda97f6_pdf

Violin Concerto No. 1, Karol Szymanowski
https://musopen.org/music/35207-violin-concerto-no1-op35/

Voice in the Wilderness, II Poco lento, Ernest Bloch
www.hyperion-records.co.uk/dw.asp?dc=W14112_67910

www.boosey.com/shop/ucat/100664?gclid=EAIaIQobChMIm
NDul6iF2wIV7r3tCh3HxAxcEAAYASAAEgKuqfD_BwE

Sources and Acknowledgement
of Illustrations

129   Jacopo Pontormo, Supper at Emmaus, Uffizi Gallery, www.commons.wikimedia.org.
134   Andrea Mantegna, Agony in the Garden, Uffizi Gallery, www.commons.wikimedia.org.
136   Photo by www.istockphoto.com, artist and location unknown.
147   Giotto, Lower Basilica, Assisi, www.commons.wikimedia.org.
149   Photo by www.istockphoto.com.
157   Photo by www.christchurchgravesend.org.uk.
167   Photo by www.istockphoto.com.
184   Photo by https://peterboroughcathedral.wordpress.com.